The Global Economic Crisis and East Asian Regionalism

Regional cooperation in East Asia on various issue areas, such as emergency liquidity mechanisms in finance, the exponential growth of free trade agreements and policy coordination on the environment and public health, developed rapidly after the Asian Financial Crisis. A decade later, the global financial crisis offered a new opportunity for the nascent regional cooperation mechanisms to acquire new depth and meaning – this time, however, in a very different context due to the unfaltering rise of China. How have inter-state cooperation mechanisms, which were devised originally to deal with the problems of the past crisis, fared in the recent global economic turbulence? Can regional integration effectively insulate East Asia from the vagaries of the international market? Should East Asian nations heed the call for *regionalism* or *globalism*?

This volume offers one of the first assessments of how the global economic crisis has affected the prospects for regional integration in East Asia. It also addresses a number of long-standing debates of interest to East Asian specialists, economists and policymakers: Are crises catalysts for revamping developmental models? Do they provide solid foundations for regional solidarity and integration? Can they help catapult countries into the global limelight?

This book was originally published as a special issue of *The Pacific Review*.

Saori N. Katada is Associate Professor at School of International Relations, University of Southern California. She is the author of *Banking on Stability* (2001), and has co-edited three books and numerous articles on trade, financial and monetary cooperation in East Asia as well as Japanese foreign aid.

The Global Economic Crisis and East Asian Regionalism

Edited by
Saori N. Katada

Routledge
Taylor & Francis Group
LONDON AND NEW YORK

First published 2012
by Routledge
2 Park Square, Milton Park, Abingdon, Oxon, OX14 4RN

Simultaneously published in the USA and Canada
by Routledge
711 Third Avenue, New York, NY 10017

Routledge is an imprint of the Taylor & Francis Group, an informa business

This book is a reproduction of *The Pacific Review*, vol. 24, issue 3. The Publisher requests to those authors who may be citing this book to state, also, the bibliographical details of the special issue on which the book was based.

British Library Cataloguing in Publication Data
A catalogue record for this book is available from the British Library

ISBN13: 978-0-415-52580-0

Typeset in Times New Roman
by Taylor & Francis Books

Publisher's Note
The publisher would like to make readers aware that the chapters in this book may be referred to as articles as they are identical to the articles published in the special issue. The publisher accepts responsibility for any inconsistencies that may have arisen in the course of preparing this volume for print.

FSC www.fsc.org MIX Paper from responsible sources FSC® C004839

Printed and bound in Great Britain by the MPG Books Group

Contents

Seeking a place for East Asian regionalism: challenges and opportunities under the global financial crisis

Saori N. Katada

Abstract After the devastating experience of the Asian financial crisis more than ten years ago, East Asia launched regional economic cooperation efforts. East Asia's mixed response to the global financial crisis a decade later, however, reveals how certain impetuses that gave rise to unified efforts to regional institution building in East Asia at the time of the AFC derived, fundamentally, from the region's defensive desire as it positioned itself within the harsh global economic and political environment of that time. The GFC triggered reorganization of global economic governance by discrediting neoliberal principles, introducing a new global governance structure and allowing reliance of domestic stimuli for economic recovery. Those shifts, in turn, led to the loss of East Asia's basic mandate towards regional cooperation. In other words, the focus of solving the region's economic vulnerability has now moved from regional arrangement to national and global stages. In particular, the East Asian governments now see less of a need to counterweight the predominant neoliberal voice through unified regional voice as the expansion of the forum to discuss global economic governance to G20 and IMF reform to provide East Asia more representation.

Saori N. Katada is Associate Professor at the School of International Relations, and also the Director of the Political Science and International Relations PhD Program (POIR) at the University of Southern California. She is the author of a book *Banking on Stability: Japan and the Cross-Pacific Dynamics of International Financial Crisis Management* (University of Michigan Press, 2001), which was awarded the Masayoshi Ohira Memorial Book Award in 2002. She also has three co-edited books: *Global Governance: Germany and Japan in International System* (Ashgate, 2004), *Cross Regional Trade Agreements: Understanding Permeated Regionalism in East Asia* (Springer, 2008), and *Competitive Regionalism: FTA Diffusion in the Pacific Rim* (Palgrave Macmillan, 2009).

Introduction

After the devastating experience of the Asian financial crisis (AFC), East Asia launched regional economic cooperation efforts about ten years ago. On the financial side, East Asian monetary authorities began their effort to establish a regional emergency funding mechanism that utilized currency swaps to fend off currency at the time of financial crises (Chiang Mai Initiative – CMI), which is structured to insulate the regional economy from the impact of financial turmoil like the AFC. Furthermore, in the face of financial globalization, economists and policy makers in the region promoted the importance of regional financial and monetary governance that address the danger of excessive reliance on foreign, particularly short-term, capital and of dollar dependence. On the trade side, despite export dependence on the extra-regional markets continuing into the 2000s, economic reform and trade liberalization imposed by the AFC opened opportunities for regional economies to move from a multilateralism-only (WTO) approach to experimenting, quite aggressively, with preferential trade arrangements (generally known as the Free Trade Agreements, FTA). Most of these FTAs are bilateral, but there has been regional effort towards a free trade area, where ASEAN has been quite successful in managing the FTA boom around it.

As shock waves of the global financial crisis (GFC) reached East Asia in autumn 2008 immediately after the collapse of Lehman Brothers in September, the region faced the task of evaluating and reassessing the economic cooperation efforts of the previous ten years. As discussed in the collection of articles in this special issue, the GFC imposed on these regional economies not only the economic hardship, but also a challenge through which economic reforms and regional cooperation efforts of the last ten years were tested. Most aptly summarized by Beeson in this special issue, the comparison of the AFC and GFC reveals that financial 'crises can have centrifugal as well as centripetal effects' on regionalism in East Asia. While the AFC spun the region into denser cooperation, Beeson notes that the GFC would impose more forces to pull the region apart due to the region's lack of effective mechanisms to coordinate collective responses. How can we understand such a dilemma in East Asia's regionalism efforts?

Grimes examines the challenge of the GFC on regional financial cooperation in general, and the most established institution in the region, the CMI, in particular. During the height of the immediate financial shock in autumn 2008, both Korea and Singapore avoided tapping CMI swap lines for liquidity support, and instead requested help from the US Federal Reserve. This was despite the very fact that East Asian monetary authorities established the facility precisely to prepare the region against a GFC-type financial crisis. Obviously, this was a major blow to the credibility of the CMI, but such a drawback was offset by the final decision in March 2009 to pool the CMI swap lines that had established a regional emergency funding facility (the so-called Chiang Mai Initiative Multilateralized – CMIM). But Grimes argues that the practical effects of multilateralization are likely to be much more limited than supporters hoped for. In particular, he argues that the challenges of surveillance and conditionality are likely to be insurmountable in the ASEN+3, thus ensuring a continuing role for the IMF. He notes that the eurozone's sovereign debt crises of 2010–11 demonstrate that even the EU has not resolved those fundamental challenges. Solís also provides evidence of a mixed picture of achievements and challenges when it comes to regional trade cooperation. Despite the call to 'rebalance' the regional trade away from heavy dependence on external markets, particularly that of the United States, the intra-regional market is still very fragmented due to protectionism and lack of a region-wide FTA that could remove trade barriers. Focusing on China, the largest economy in the region and the second largest in the world (since mid 2010), Jiang argues that recent economic stimulus packages implemented by the Chinese government focus on the old style, state-led model of economic growth. These place strong emphasis on low-cost, labor-intensive, export-centric manufacturing, which opens limited space for regional economic integration.

East Asia's mixed response to the GFC reveals how certain impetuses that gave rise to 'centripetal' regional institution-building efforts in East Asia at the time of the AFC derived fundamentally from the region's defensive desire, as it positioned itself within the harsh global economic and political environment of that time. Therefore, once the GFC shifted the ground and accommodated challenges that engendered regional cooperation, it weakened the governments' efforts to cooperate.

As discussed in detail below, the first impetus arises from the ideational clash between East Asia's economic model and economic neoliberalism predominantly seen in the IMF prescriptions to various financial crises behind financial globalization and push towards trade liberalization. The second set contains the fundamentals of the region's economic management as these economies liberalize and globalize. Regional arrangements both in finance and trade came as a way to balance two competing economic demands in the region; one side comes from remaining developmental state elements embedded strongly in domestic interests, and the other from global economic players in the region in pursuit of larger gains and efficiency. Finally and most centrally, the rise of regionalism in East Asia came as a counterweight strategy for the region as it pursues legitimacy and voice without confronting head-on the global economic governance debate dominated by the United States.

This article argues, in short, that the GFC triggered reorganization of global economic governance by discrediting neoliberal principles, introducing a new global governance structure and allowing reliance of domestic stimuli for economic recovery. Those shifts, in turn, led to the loss of East Asia's basic mandate towards regional cooperation. In other words, the focus of solving the region's economic vulnerability has moved from regional arrangement to national and global stages. In particular, the East Asian governments now see less of a need to counterweight the predominant neoliberal voice through unified regional voice, as the new G20 has provided East Asia more representation in global economic governance and the IMF reforms.

This article is structured as follows: the first section summarizes existing work in three sets of perspectives regarding what gave rise to regionalism in post-AFC East Asia. The second section lays out the rhetoric and reality of East Asia's regional cooperation and institutional building since the GFC, and finally, the last section analyzes how and why East Asia's regional cooperation has been affected by the changes in global economic governance triggered by the GFC.

East Asia in the global economy: the region's pursuit of regionalism after the AFC

Very few dispute the assertion that the AFC was *the* watershed event for East Asia that set off multiple movements towards regional institution building, particularly in the area of finance, but also in other areas, including trade. The fundamental challenge for East Asia at that time was how to survive the crisis and safeguard the region from future crises. At the domestic level, multiple measures have since been taken: a dramatic increase in exports (Ravenhill 2008) with effective corporate governance (Gourevitch 2008) on one hand, and prudent financial management and (partial) compliance with international financial standard at the domestic level (Walter 2008; Hamilton-Hart 2008), as well as efforts in nurturing domestic bond markets to reduce excessive dependence on banks (Amyx 2008), on the other. Many countries in the region also accumulated a massive amount of foreign exchange reserves to insulate their economies from financial and exchange rate volatility (Mohanty and Turner 2006).

What is striking, however, is the visible regional and institutional reaction in the aftermath of the crisis. The question, then, is what prompted the East Asian leaders to devise *regional* response? What were/are the goals of regional cooperation that cannot be obtained nationally? Of course, each government has different objectives, and some of the objectives of large countries (such as Japan and China) contrast with those of the smaller ones. In addition, East Asia houses diverse countries in terms of the level of development (and its associated aspects such as technical and governance capacities), political institutions (democratic versus non-democratic), as well as the sentiment for and against the United States and about each other. Therefore, one might wonder; what is achieved by joining together regionally or institutionalizing economic arrangements that were informal before the AFC? Scholars put forth three strands of answers to the question.

First, and quite often discussed, motivation behind East Asia's regional turn, especially in the area of finance, emerges from the ideological clash between the Asia leaders and the '(IMF-)Wall Street-Treasury' complex (Bhagwati 1998; Wade and Veneroso 1998) in the face of the AFC. Discrediting the economic model that allegedly made East Asia an economic miracle was at stake. The crisis gave the 'Washington Consensus' economists analytical and policy ammunition to argue that the Asian way of economic management was, at a fundamental level, flawed, and the failure of the model had contributed to this crisis (Hall 2003). Active debates at the time centered on whether the AFC was a crisis of fundamentals arising from East Asia's failed economic management or that of temporary liquidity crisis.[1] The 'fundamental camp', rooted in neoliberalist economic view, went further and blamed both the corrupt and often inefficient 'crony capitalism' of many Asian economies and demanded those countries engage in dramatic economic reform in compliance with international regulatory norms of corporate governance and transparency. On the other hand, East Asia's 'liquidity camp', popular with Asian economists and policy makers, blamed premature and excessive liberalization in finance and the global financial architecture for allowing rapid and massive inflow and outflow of foreign capital into Asia, leading to the temporary imbalance, and demanded reform in the international financial architecture to regulate those so-called highly leveraged institutions (HLIs) such as hedge funds (Yoshitomi and Ohno 1999; Sakakibara 2000).

The proposal by the Japanese government to establish the Asian Monetary Fund (AMF) at the height of the AFC, argues Lee (2006), emerged from Japan's ideational position on the course of economic development, deriving from its own developmental experiences. Although this proposal was rejected by the United States and IMF, and did not please China (Amyx 2005) at that point, China gradually warmed up to the idea of a regional emergency funding mechanism (CMI) (Chey 2009). Moreover, many of the countries directly hit by the AFC, and having to endure the IMF conditionality, engaged in a so-called 'politics of resentment' (Higgott 1998), where the countries' leadership shifted blame for the crisis to outside influence as they scrambled to justify their economic policies.

In short, the common experience of the AFC created a psychological bond among East Asian leaders and policy makers. The crisis not only triggered the development of active communication networks among the financial policy makers across the region, but it also allowed the entire population to share the 'common other' in the form of the IMF and the Western financiers, entities which became the target of criticism and blame and united Asia (Terada 2003). As the East Asian economies became mired by economic, political and social crises, the demanding and triumphant attitude of the Washington Consensus took on a revolting appearance.[2] Such collective regional identity did not immediately form in the area of trade. Nonetheless, the collaborative atmosphere created in the aftermath of the crisis also encouraged discussion toward an FTA. Even the countries such as South Korea and Japan, which had thus far seen themselves as trade rivals, began the FTA studies as proposed by the Korean then-President Kim Dae Jung at the time of his visit to Tokyo in autumn 1998.

Focusing on materialist interests, the second set of arguments analyzes the rise of East Asian regionalism from economic grounds. This can be divided into three sources. The first source was the common or similar challenges that the region faced in terms of economic 'growing pains' under the intense pressure of economic globalization in the 1990s. As many economies in the region advanced through export-led industrialization, economic success turned into a challenge of phasing out developmentalist policies (Bauer 1992, for example). This post-Cold War 1990s was characterized not only by the increasing protectionism against East Asian exports in Asia's largest market, the United States, but also by mounting pressures, directly from the United States and indirectly through other multilateral processes, to liberalize the economies of the region both in trade and finance. The difficulty of surviving these challenges culminated in the AFC, where the missteps such as premature financial liberalization and chronic trade account deficit (both especially in the case of Thailand), and a deficiency in the government's oversight of the private corporations' financial behavior (such as the case for South Korea), triggered the spiraling crisis.

The AFC revealed the region's second source of challenges, which is the vulnerability of the deep interdependence and interconnectedness among East Asian economies, developed over the course of a successful 'economic regionalization' that linked the regional economies with regional production networks and ethnic Chinese business networks since the 1980s (Peng 2002). Despite the intensity of such informal and business-led integration, few realized before the crisis the common economic fate such linkage has brought about for the region. As the currency crisis in Thailand rattled almost all the open East Asian economies within a few days, the fear of contagion spread through the region and beyond. Despite variation in the severity of the crisis, it is commonly understood that the region overall (with the possible exception of closed countries such as North Korea) was affected (Noble and Ravenhill 2000). The implication is that whether each country wants it or not, it has to consider regional economic stability as collective good.

Finally, a common regional fate also arises from across-the-board reliance on the external market for its final products, currency and finance. The dollar dependence was critically important where the very pegging of Thai baht trigged the AFC in the first place, and many of the East Asian economies had to depeg and subsequently suffer a dramatic devaluation of their own currencies against the dollar (in 1997). Furthermore, a part of regional contagion was arguably from the competitive devaluation of Southeast Asian currencies against the dollar as each country struggled to 'export its way out of the crisis'. In this environment, ASEAN members had to become serious about their trade integration efforts, with the aim to attract more foreign direct investment. Not only did then-ASEAN Secretary-General Severinto announce the region's commitment to integration, it was also decided to accelerate the speed of the AFTA tariff liberalization schedule in 1998 (Bowles 2000: 443–4).

In sum, one can argue that the post-AFC regional response emerged from the leaders' profound realization regarding the regional economic challenges. Although many of these countries pursued national strategies to recover from the crisis with massive exports and prepare itself against the next possible foreign exchange shock by accumulating foreign exchange reserves, regional economic readiness surfaced as one of the policy priorities.

The third set of motivations to collaborate regionally emerges from East Asia's frustration at not having enough 'voice opportunity' (Grieco 1995) with regard to global economic governance. First and foremost, at the time of the AFC, the region's policy makers were shocked to find that they did not have any regional recourse as they faced the task of dealing with the crisis. ASEAN was not strong enough and APEC was too diverse to find a solution to the crisis (Webber 2001); the Asian Development Bank (ADB) responded only timidly and inconsistently to the task of being the regional lender of last resort (Wesley 1999). Furthermore, the central bankers in the region has set up Executives' Meeting of East Asia and Pacific Central Banks (EMEAP) since 1991, but the institution has had limited influence on regional cooperation due to the secrecy of the meetings and lack of institutional commitment to coordinate supervisory influence (Yokoi-Arai 2006: 55). In the end, some East Asian governments had to turn to the IMF, whose available funding was considered not enough to address the crisis due to the relatively small quotas that East Asian countries were assigned (Rapkin and Strand 2003). Furthermore, in relation to their relatively small quotas, the voting shares of the Asian countries in the institution were limited (Sohn 2005).

Increasing East Asia's global political influence, however, has never been an easy feat. The Japanese government had been pushing for its quota increase for a few decades before the AFC to manage to become the second largest quota holder at the IMF. But its voice has not been sufficiently reflected in IMF policies or those of the World Bank. Wade (1996) argues that Japan's lack of influence is attributed to the entrenched neoliberal paradigm prevalent in those institutions, and its voice also fell short at the time of the AFC (Lee 2006). In addition, given its security and economic dependence, it has always been difficult for Japan to confront directly the US dominance in the international financial institutions (IFIs). Even at the height of the AFC, Japan's position was ambivalent. On the one hand, it was ready to cooperate with the United States in taking care of East Asia's economic needs under the crisis, but on the other, some Japanese policy makers resented its inability to take leadership in addressing the Asian path to crisis management (Sakakibara 2000, for example). Emerging China was not yet willing to pay a significant price to enhance its political influence in the global economy despite some signs of it becoming a 'responsible stakeholder' as its government maintained the value of its currency at the time of the crisis without engaging in competitive devaluation with the Southeast Asian countries. In this context, collective efforts in East Asia began to prepare the region against similar crisis, and the countries also established some 'counterweight' in getting their collective voice heard in the international arena (Katada 2004; Sohn 2007).[3] Hence, helped by the common experience of the AFC, and with the realization of the region's economic vulnerability, most of the East Asian economies gradually began to cultivate a common regional position despite a variety of capital account positions and types of domestic financial governance (Hiwatari 2003).

Counterweight strategy appears in the form of standard-setting competition in the field of FTA policy. In the competitive world of the FTA race, large countries like Japan, China and the United States have engaged in rule-setting competition. For East Asia, in particular, the insertion of competitive policy and ways to circumvent anti-dumping lawsuits from the United States and Europe through special rules on trade remedies, became pillars of bilateral FTA policies (Nakagawa 2009: 80).

Furthermore, thanks to the newly established Asia Europe Meeting (ASEM) since 1996, there was a forum for East Asia to unify its voice in preparation to discuss various issues with the European Union in the ASEM summits held every other year. This forum successfully excluded the United States from Asian affairs for the first time (Bobrow 1999), and there they discussed the agendas important to Europe, such as the future of common currencies (Katada 2004; Gilson 1999).

Overall, there is no doubt the AFC had a profound impact on the economic and policy priorities in East Asia from ideational, economic and political grounds. The regional turn was facilitated by all the three sources.

Post-GFC East Asian regionalism: rhetoric and reality

During the decade since the AFC, economic cooperation in East Asia has intensified. The analyses of the real economy (Park and Shin 2009) and macroeconomic indicators (Kawai and Motonishi 2005) appear to suggest that, by intensifying intra-regional trade along with the careful macroeconomic and financial management, East Asia has finally managed to 'decouple' itself from the American-dominated global economy. Such triumphalism of East Asian integration has been heard clearly since the subprime mortgage crisis began to rattle the economies of the United States and Europe in late 2007 (Mahbubani 2008). The global economic picture, however, looks incongruous from the other side of the Pacific: the actual way in which East Asia recovered from the AFC increased external dependence through trade, and it has led to the criticism of so-called 'global imbalance' as East Asia accumulated its current account surplus (particularly against the United States) and high savings. In contrast, the United States piled up its trade and budget deficits, which also allegedly created the macroeconomic environment for the subprime mortgage crisis there (Bernanke 2005; Wolf 2008).

The optimism of East Asia being saved from the economic downturn did not last long. In the immediate aftermath of the Lehman shock in autumn 2008, contraction of extra-regional export of final products led to a dramatic decline of intra-regional intra-firm component trade (Goldstein and Xie 2009), leading to a 6–38% quarterly drop in exports from East Asian countries in the last quarter of 2008 and the first quarter of 2009 (Ahn 2010). In this way, the American and European economic crisis was transmitted through the trade channel.

Facing this economic challenge, Asian policy makers began to advocate 'rebalancing' of the region's economic dependence away from exports and towards production for domestic markets (ADB 2009). Thus, the urgent need for an alternative to the United States market granted East Asia an opportunity to call for an upgrade of mostly bilateral FTAs in the region to a region-wide free trade area. The manufacturing industries in East Asia would benefit significantly from having such a region-wide FTA. This would allow the region to obtain much larger economies of scale and avoid cumbersome rules of origin (ROO) specific to each bilateral FTA, particularly since component trade across borders multiplies the transaction costs of tariffs and procedures to clear ROO are cumbersome.

Furthermore, the US-originated global financial crisis profoundly shook confidence in the dollar among the monetary authorities in the region and triggered anxiety over the economies' overexposure in various forms. Such overdependence and lack of alternatives made the regional monetary authorities very uncomfortable. Addressing such concern, the Governor of the People's Bank of China, Zhou Xiaochuan (2009), argued in favor of international monetary reform and increased use of special drawing rights (SDR) in order to supplement or supplant the dominant role of the dollar as the international key currency. At the same time, the Chinese government signed several currency swaps in RMB with countries that had large trade payments to China, a move which has incurred suspicion that China is on the way to launch a currency offensive.[4] The regional currency architecture gained strategic salience in Japan too as the former Prime Minister Nakasone began to urge a common currency area in East Asia (Nakasone 2009). Furthermore, the first Democratic Party (DPJ) Prime Minister Hatoyama, sworn in after the Liberal Democratic Party (LDP) defeat in summer of 2009, emphasized his aspiration to create a common currency in Asia as a way to reduce the region's external dependence (Hatoyama 2009). Needless to say, there has yet to emerge a consensus as to how such a common currency would operate, and the scheme has not yet gained support from the central bankers in the region.

The rise in regionalism rhetoric was also supported by the fact that America's insistence on and belief in the unregulated financial market was shaken by the crisis. Even the almighty guardian of neoliberalism, the former Fed Chairman Alan Greenspan, came forward to admit the he found 'a flaw' in the free-market model (House Committee on Oversight and Government Reform 2008). These changes in the economic atmosphere, and increased interest in regional economic insulation against the on-going crisis, should, one would expect, boost the push toward stronger regionalism initiatives. As Grimes and Solís discuss in their respective articles, however, the records in both financial and trade regionalism efforts in the face of the GFC have been mixed at best.

In the area of finance, the GFC, from autumn 2008 to spring 2009, simultaneously promoted and damaged the CMI process. As discussed by Grimes, the visible damage the GFC inflicted on the credibility of the CMI came from the fact that South Korea and Singapore, when faced with a severe liquidity crisis in autumn 2008, did not resort to the CMI. The Korean government, instead, went to the US Federal Reserve at the end of October with its request for $30 billion in swap lines (Aizenman et al. 2010). Although the Korean monetary authority's reasons for avoiding the CMI are not clear, their reluctance at the time of the crisis put a dent in the credibility of the CMI process, which had never been activated thus far, and essentially confirmed the difficulty in resorting to the CMI.

In contrast, the GFC gave a noticeable lift to the leaders who were dragging their feet when it came to the multilateralizing of the CMI process. The GFC facilitated agreement on the amount of contribution to the mechanism by the two major powers in the region, Japan and China, and the Korean government's decision *not* to utilize the CMI strengthened the conviction of CMI members to enhance economic monitoring (and with its success further reduction of the IMF link). These agreements were reached in early 2009, and the CMIM, which consists of a multilateral swap agreement among the member central banks with pooled fund of $120 billion (in US dollars), came into effect on 24 March 2010.[5] Through the multilateralization process, not only did the CMIM expand the available amount of swaps, but it also allowed ASEAN countries (namely Brunei, Cambodia, Laos and Vietnam) that were not previously connected by the bilateral swaps to become full members of the CMI process.

Regarding the currency, the GFC exposed the double-edged nature of East Asia's reliance on the US dollar. The region escaped an AFC-type currency crisis this time partly thanks to a huge accumulation of foreign exchange reserves, particularly in dollars, in the region, where China reports $2.5 trillion (March 2010) and Japan $1.04 trillion (April 2010) in reserves. But despite many post-AFC policy dialogues and studies done on the desirability of reducing East Asia's dollar dependence, the region actually *increased* its exposure to this key currency in the last ten years between the AFC and GFC (Katada 2008).[6] In addition, the lack of common agreement about the region's currency direction, and power plays on the matter are also demonstrated in the way that Japan and China independently came to Korea's (too-little too-late) 'rescue' in the context of +3 meeting in December 2008, as each pledged increased bilateral swap lines to Korea in their own currencies. The Japan–Korea swap (yen and won) was increased from the equivalent of $3 billion to the equivalent of $20 billion and the +3 countries announced the establishment of a new China–Korea swap equivalent to $26 billion (RMB and won).

In trade, Solís discusses the mushrooming of new FTAs in East Asia. By autumn 2009, East Asia concluded 37 FTAs, with 40 more under negotiation and an additional 26 proposed, in comparison to 2000 in which there were three concluded, one under negotiation and two proposed (Kawai and Wignaraja 2009: Appendix Table 2). Most of those FTAs are bilateral, and quite a large number of them are cross-regional (Solís and Katada 2007), while the most important bilateral trade links within East Asia (such as Japan–China) have not been covered. Furthermore, the complex implementation of ROO associated with the numerous bilateral FTAs crisscrossing the region and beyond (the so-called 'noodle bowl') makes use of FTA provisions cumbersome, and lowers the utilization rates of tariff concession through these FTAs to an estimated 5–20% (Takahashi and Urata 2008). Despite various proposals to establish region-wide FTAs and even with the pressing 'rebalancing' needs, there has been no convergence on membership and framework among those region-wide efforts, such as CEPEA (Comprehensive Economic Partnership for East Asia with 16 ASEAN+6 countries) and EAFTA (East Asia Free Trade Area with 13 ASEAN+3 countries) (Kawai and Wignaraja 2008). Such a fragmented FTA network in East Asia is curious in the face of increased intra-regional trade and regional production networks that created a highly integrated regional economy (Munakata 2006).

In sum, as Beeson also notes, East Asia's regionalism efforts did not bloom in the same way under the GFC as they did under the AFC. The interesting question here is why is this so, and what does such lack of momentum in the most recent crisis tell us about the nature of East Asian regionalism?

The shifting ground for East Asian regionalism

The GFC, particularly after the Lehman shock, seemed like a perfect opportunity to move East Asia's regionalism forward. The neoliberal economic paradigm was clearly discredited. The financial and economic governance forum was expanded from the exclusive Atlantic-centric G7 to the G20 that includes four East Asian countries (Japan, China, South Korea and Indonesia) in the summitry discussion at the global level,[7] and IMF quota-and-voting-share reform kicked off to reflect the increasing economic weight of East Asia is on the table. Furthermore, despite some initial economic shock, East Asia experienced a swift recovery from the economic downturn just one year later (World Bank 2010). Thus far, however, East Asia's regional cooperation has not picked up its pace, as the GFC has pulled the region in the direction of a global and nation-centric recovery instead of a regional one.

As discussed above, the foundation of *regional* efforts in finance and trade emerged from the region's ideational, economic and political needs that were profoundly felt in the aftermath of the AFC. Those efforts started at the time when neoliberalist ideas and policies dominated the global economic governance, and there was little political influence available to the East Asian countries either individually or collectively. Shocks from the GFC shifted such ideological grounds and conditions, and the overwhelming predominance of neoliberalism has waned. One indication of this shifting tide has been the strong call for government regulations and oversight of the financial institutions and transactions in order to avoid a recurrence of excessive risk taking. Discussions over international financial regulatory reforms have progressed with energy from 2008 to 2010 at the G20, as well as at the Financial Stability Board (Helleiner and Pagliari 2010).[8] Such a shifting tide of economic principles is also visible as the IMF, the guardian of financial liberalization, openly acknowledged the risk of free capital movement and the usefulness of capital control (IMF 2010).

Economic policies in response to the GFC were also in line with what East Asia would have wanted at the time of the AFC (but could not achieve). Following the strategies of the United States and European countries to boost their economies with massive fiscal stimulus packages in response to the financial crisis, East Asian governments also opted to engage in domestic stimuli after their dramatic contraction from late 2008. On top of China's well-known $586 billion stimulus package, boosting the economy with nearly 14% of the country's GDP, almost all East Asian countries injected fiscal stimuli to their respective economies, amounting to from 2–9% of GDP, and implemented monetary easing (ADB 2008: 15–17).[9] But such a national recovery strategy did not cater to increased regional integration especially in the field of trade. Even though the smooth recovery of China's growth rate and its domestic consumption allowed some Asian economies to enjoy a V-shaped economic recovery by late 2009 and early 2010 (ADB 2010), as Jiang emphasizes in this special issue, the Chinese economic recovery policy focused on the old developmental state model with the emphasis on exporting (to the United States) its way out of the crisis; a clear indication that China has no intention of weaning itself from its reliance on the US market any time soon. Beyond China and despite efforts to keep the protectionist upsurge in check under this recession (Gamberoni and Newfarmer 2009), liberalizing trade at a time of economic uncertainty has been a political hard sell. Such a tendency is exacerbated by the very political nature of trade policy making among the large economies of East Asia, such as Japan and Korea, where opposition from anti-trade groups, like agriculture, tends to weigh heavily in the countries' FTA strategies (Koo 2009; Solís 2009).

Moreover, it is quite ironic then that China resists depegging and appreciation of the RMB against the US dollar to protect the country's access to the US export market, while such close pegging of the RMB not only makes China less likely to become the currency leader in the near future, and it also allows East Asia, which now has very high level of trade with China, to maintain the de facto dollar standard.

Finally, there is no doubt that the newly introduced summitry of the global economic governance forum at G20 has brought the critical 'voice opportunity' for individual countries in East Asia.[10] Times have changed from when Japan was the only Asian representative at G7 summits and finance ministers meetings. Now, as President Hu announced at the Toronto Summit, China is willing to use the G20 as 'a premier platform for advancing international economic cooperation', to establish a 'fair, equitable, inclusive and well-managed' international financial order (Xinhua News Agency 2010). Furthermore, as the host of the G20 summit in Seoul (November 2010), the Korean government pushed the IMF reform agenda agreed on during the Pittsburgh G20 one year earlier to expand the emerging market countries' voting share at the IMF by 5% by 2011.

This shift collapsed the 'counterweight' motivation behind regional cooperation efforts in this area for Japan and East Asia; thus the participation of these Asian countries at G20, ironically, reduces the need for a regional forum to establish a collective Asian voice (Emmers and Ravenhill 2010).

Conclusion

The ideational shift and domestic stimulus-centered economic recovery strategy are victories for East Asia, and this paradigm shift was what the region sincerely yearned for at the time of the AFC more than ten years ago. As the global economic governance altered fundamentally under the GFC, however, East Asia's desire for regional cooperation seems to have lost energy. On the financial side, the shifting of the power center from G7 to G20, which includes many major East Asian governments, has weakened the need for the region to unite in hopes of establishing a strong, united front to demand the Asian voice be reflected in the global discussion. On the trade side, the fact that most recovery measures were taken nationally diminished at least for the time being the push for region-wide trade liberalization despite the desire of many integrationists to emphasize 'rebalancing' the regional economy through intra-regional trade.

Of course, those temporary setbacks do not mean the inevitable waning of regional cooperation and integration efforts in East Asia in the medium and long term. Regional institutions such as the CMIM and discussions towards regional free trade arrangements will continue to support these efforts. What is ironic at this stage, however, is having been given a more prominent place in the global economic governance after ten years of hard work, the East Asian governments seem to have lost their collective voice to celebrate.

Notes

1 A similar discussion on the cause of the AFC proceeded among the economists in the United States. The controversy is best summarized by the contrast between Radelet and Sachs (1998) emphasizing the panic-stricken behavior of domestic and international investors and the failure of the IMF response on the one hand, and Roubini emphasizing the economic distortions among the countries in Asia and the problems of fundamentals (Corsettti et al. 1999) on the other.
2 In that context, then-Malaysian Prime Minister Mahathir's attack on Soros was a good example. Meanwhile a picture of the then-IMF Managing Director Michel Camdessus standing arrogantly tall and cross-armed by the side of Indonesian President Suharto as he signed the IMF agreement under pressure from all sides in January 1998 was seen by many Asian media to signify the continuing colonial attitude of the IMF (Budianta 2000).
3 Focusing on the Japanese strategy towards international financial architecture in the aftermath of the AFC, Katada (2004; 176–7) defines that counterweight 'strategy involves a mixture of bargaining plus institution and coalition building efforts designed to increase regional and international support for Japan's position, particularly when these contrast with the U.S. position'.
4 Those swaps include Argentina (RMB 70), Belarus (RMB 20), Hong Kong (RMB 200), Indonesia (RMB 100), Korea (RMB 180) and Malaysia (RMB 80).
5 The currency swap arrangements are based on the contractual agreement among the central banks to activate those swaps based on their respective foreign exchange reserves as the CMIM receives requests. In this sense, it is not really a 'fund' that keeps certain level of quota pooled under a multilateral umbrella.
6 This incurred discussion of 'Bretton Woods II' or revived dollar-standard among the economists (Dooley et al. 2003), where the dollar remains key currency in East Asia as the economies are interested in pursuing a mercantilist policy of trade expansion rather than currency autonomy.
7 India, though not an ASEAN + 3 member, is a G20 member. In addition, the ASEAN secretariat is also invited as an observer.
8 In the last two years, four G20 summits were held in Washington DC (November 2008), London (April 2009), Pittsburgh (September 2009), and Toronto (June 2010). Their respective leaders' declarations have become increasingly long and more specific. All are available online at http://www.g20.org/pub_communiques.aspx/
9 Updated summaries of economic stimulus packages by the East Asian governments are also available from the United Nations Economic and Social Commission for Asia and the Pacific (ESCAP) at http://www.unescap.org/pdd/publications/survey2009/stimulus/fiscal-stimulus.pdf
10 The G20 was established in 1999 at the G7 Koln Summit that discussed the post-AFC global financial architecture, and the countries' financial ministers have met annually in the G20 context since then. But the arrangement did not become the core of financial discussion until 2008.

References

Ahn, C. Y. (2010) 'Weathering the storm: the impact of the global financial crisis on Asia', *Global Asia* 5(1): 58–68.

Aizenman, J., Jinjarak, Y. and Park, D. (2010) 'International reserves and swap lines: substitutes or complements', *NBER Working Paper* no. w15804.

Amyx, J. (2005) 'What motivates regional financial cooperation in East Asia today?', *Asia Pacific Issues* 76(February): 1–8.

Amyx, J. (2008) 'Regional financial cooperation in East Asia since the Asian financial crisis', in A. MacIntyre, T. J. Pempel and J. Ravenhil (eds) *Crisis as Catalyst: Asia's Dynamic Political Economy*, Ithaca, NY: Cornell University Press, pp. 117–39.

Asian Development Bank (ADB) (2008) *Asian Economic Monitor* (December), Manila: ADB.

Asian Development Bank (ADB) (2009) *Asian Development Outlook: Rebalancing Asia's Growth*, Manila: ADB.

Asian Development Bank (ADB) (2010) *Asian Development Outlook: Macroeconomic Management beyond the Crisis*, Manila: ADB.

Bauer, J. (1992) 'Industrial restructuring in the NIES: prospects and challenges', *Asian Survey* 32(11): 1012–25.

Bernanke, B. (2005) 'The global saving glut and the U.S. current account deficit', 10 March, accessed at http://www.federalreserve.gov/boarddocs/speeches/2005/200503102/default.htm. [Accessed 20 August, 2010].

Bhagwati, J. (1998) 'The capital myth: the difference between trade in widgets and dollars', *Foreign Affairs* 77(3): 7–12.

Bobrow, D. B. (1999) 'The U.S. and ASEM: why the hegemon didn't bark', *The Pacific Review* 12(1): 103–28.

Bowles, P. 2000. 'Regionalism and development after (?) the global financial crises', *New Political Economy* 5(1): 433–57.

Budianta, M. (2000) 'Discourse of cultural identity in Indonesia during the 1997–1998 monetary crisis', *Inter-Asia Cultural Studies* 1(1): 109–28.

Chey, H. (2009) 'The changing political dynamics of East Asian financial cooperation: the Chiang Mai Initiative', *Asian Survey* 49(3): 450–67.

Corsetti, G., Pesenti, P. and Roubini, N. (1999) 'What caused the Asian currency and financial crisis?',*Japan and the World Economy* 11: 305–75.

Dooley, M., Folkerts-Landau, D. and Garber, P. (2003) 'An essay on the revived Bretton Woods system', *NBER Working Paper*, no. 9971.

Emmers, R. and Ravenhill, J. (2010) 'The Asian and global financial crises: consequences for East Asian regionalism', *RSIS Working Paper*, no. 208.

Gamberoni, E. and Newfarmer, R. (2009) 'Trade protection: incipient but worrisome trend', Vox, 4 March, accessed at http://www.voxeu.org/index.php?q=node/3183. [Accessed 15 May 2010].

Gilson, J. (1999) 'Japan's role in the Asia-Europe meeting: establishing an interregional or intraregional agenda?', *Asian Survey* 39(5): 736–52.

Goldstein, M. and Xie, D. (2009) 'Impact of financial crisis on emerging Asia', *Peterson Institute for International Economics*, Working Paper, 09-11.

Gourevitch, P. (2008) 'Containing the oligarchs: the politics of corporate governance systems in East Asia', in A. MacIntyre, T. J. Pempel and J. Ravenhil (eds) *Crisis as Catalyst: Asia's Dynamic Political Economy*, Ithaca, NY: Cornell University Press, pp. 70–92.

Grieco, J. M. (1995) 'The Maastricht Treaty: economic and monetary union and the neo-realist research programme', *Review of International Studies* 21(1): 21–40.

Hall, R. (2003) 'The discursive demolition of the Asian development model', *International Studies Quarterly* 47: 71–99.

Hamilton-Hart, N. (2008) 'Banking systems a decade after the crisis', in A. MacIntyre, T. J. Pempel and J. Ravenhill (eds) *Crisis as Catalyst: Asia's Dynamic Political Economy*, Ithaca, NY: Cornell University Press, pp. 45–69.

Hatoyama, Y. (2009) 'My political philosophy', *Voice*, September, accessed at http://www.hatoyama.gr.jp/masscomm/090810.html. [Accessed 10 October 2010].

Helleiner, E. and Pagliari, S. (2010) 'Crisis and reform of international financial regulation', in E. Helleiner, S. Pagliari and H. Zimmermann (eds) *Global Finance in Crisis: The Politics of International Regulatory Change*, New York: Routledge, pp. 1–18.

Higgott, R. (1998) 'The Asian economic crisis: a study in the politics of resentment', *New Political Economy* 3(3): 333–56.

Hiwatari, N. (2003) 'Embedded policy preferences and the formation of international arrangements after the Asian financial crisis', *The Pacific Review* 16(3): 331–59.

House Committee on Oversight and Government Reform. 2008. *Hearing of the House Committee on Oversight and Government Reform Subject: The Financial Crisis and the Role of Federal Regulators*, October 23, 2008.

International Monetary Fund (IMF) (2010) 'Capital inflows: the role of controls', *IMF Staff Position Note* SPN/10/04, 19 February.

Katada, S. N. (2004) 'Japan's counterweight strategy: U.S.–Japan cooperation and competition in international finance', in S. K. Ellis and T. J. Pempel (eds) *Beyond Bilateralism: U.S.–Japan Relations in the New Asia-Pacific*, Palo Alto, CA: Stanford University Press, pp. 176–97.

Katada, S. N. (2008) 'From a supporter to a challenger? Japan's currency leadership in dollar-dominated East Asia', *Review of International Political Economy* 15(3): 399–417.

Kawai, M. and Motonishi, T. (2005) 'Macroeconomic interdependence in East Asia: empirical evidence and issues', in Asian Development Bank (ed.) *Asian Cooperation and Integration: Progress, Prospects, Challenges*, Manila: Asian Development Bank, pp. 213–68.

Kawai, M. and Wignaraja, G. (2008) 'EAFTA or CEPEA: which way forward?', *ASEAN Economic Bulletin* 25(2): 113–39.

Kawai, M. and Wignaraja, G. (2009) 'Asian FTAs: trends and challenges', *ADBI Working Paper Series*, no. 144, August.

Koo, M. G. (2009) 'South Korea's FTAs: moving from an emulative to a competitive strategy', in M. Solís, B. Stallings and S. N. Katada (eds) *Competitive Regionalism: FTA Diffusion in the Pacific Rim*, London: Palgrave, pp. 181–97.

Lee, Y. W. (2006) 'Japan and the Asian Monetary Fund: an identity-intention approach', *International Studies Quarterly* 50(2): 339–66.

Mahbubani, K. (2008) 'Why Asia stays calm in the storm', *Financial Times*, 28 October.

Mohanty, M. S. and Turner, P. (2006) 'Foreign exchange reserve accumulation in emerging markets: what are the domestic implications?', *BIS Quarterly Bulletin* (September): 39–52.

Munakata, N. (2006) 'Has politics caught up with the markets? In search of East Asian economic regionalism', in P. J. Katzenstein and T. Shiraishi (eds) *Beyond Japan: The Dynamics of East Asian Regionalism*, Ithaca, NY: Cornell University Press, pp. 130–57.

Nakagawa, J. (2009) 'Competitive regionalism through bilateral and regional rule-making: standard setting and locking-in', in M. Solís, B. Stallings and S. N.

Katada (eds) *Competitive Regionalism: FTA Diffusion in the Pacific Rim*, London: Palgrave, pp. 74–95.

Nakasone, Yasuhiro (2009) 'Kyotsu tsuka ga hiraku nihon to ajia no mirai' [The future of Japan and East Asia opened up by the common currency], *Chuo koron* (April): 182–93.

Noble, G. and Ravenhill, J. (2000) 'Causes and consequences of the Asian financial crisis', in G. Noble and J. Ravenhill (eds) *The Asian Financial Crisis and the Architecture of Global Finance*, Cambridge: Cambridge University Press, pp. 1–35.

Park, Y. C. and Shin, K. (2009) 'Economic integration and changes in the business cycle in East Asia: is the region decoupling from the rest of the world', *Asian Economic Papers* 8(2): 107–40.

Peng, D. (2002) 'Invisible linkages: a regional perspective of East Asian political economy', *International Studies Quarterly* 46(3): 423–47.

Radelet, S. and Sachs, J. (1998) 'The East Asian financial crisis: diagnosis, remedies, prospects', *Brookings Papers on Economic Activity* 1: 1–90.

Rapkin, D. P. and Strand, J. R. (2003) 'Is East Asia Under-represented in the International Monetary Fund?', *International Relations of the Asia Pacific* 3: 1–28.

Ravenhill, J. (2008) 'Trading out of the crisis', in A. MacIntyre, T. J. Pempel and J. Ravenhill (eds) *Crisis as Catalyst: Asia's Dynamic Political Economy*, Ithaca, NY: Cornell University Press, pp. 140–63.

Sakakibara, Eisuke (2000) *Nihon to Sekai ga Furueta Hi: Saiba Shinhonsyugi no Seritsu* [The Day when Japan and the World Shuddered: The Establishment of Cyber Capitalism], Tokyo: Chuo Korensha.

Sohn, I. (2005) 'Asian financial cooperation: the problem of legitimacy in global financial governance', *Global Governance* 11(4): 487–504.

Sohn, I. (2007). 'East Asia's counterweight strategy: Asian financial cooperation and evolving international monetary order', *G-24 Discussion Paper Series*, no. 44, March.

Solís, M. (2009) 'Japan's competitive FTA strategy: commercial opportunity versus political rivalry', in M. Solís, B. Stallings and S. N. Katada (eds) *Competitive Regionalism: FTA Diffusion in the Pacific Rim*, London: Palgrave, pp. 198–215.

Solís, M. and Katada, S. N. (2007). 'Understanding East Asian cross-regionalism: an analytical framework', *Pacific Affairs* 80(2): 229–57.

Takahashi, K. and Urata, S. (2008) 'On the use of FTAs by Japanese firms', *RIETI Discussion Paper* 08-E-002.

Terada, Ti. (2003) 'Constructing an "East Asian" concept and growing regional identity: from EAEC to ASEAN+3', *The Pacific Review* 16(2): 251–77.

Wade, R. (1996) 'Japan, the World Bank, and the art of paradigm maintenance: the East Asian miracle in political perspective', *New Left Review* (May/June): 3–36.

Wade, R. and Veneroso, F. (1998) 'The Asian crisis: the high debt model versus the Wall Street treasury IMF complex', *New Left Review* (March/April): 3–22.

Walter, A. (2008) *Governing Finance: East Asia's Adoption of International Standard*, Ithaca, NY: Cornell University Press.

Webber, D. (2001) 'Two funerals and a wedding? The ups and downs of regionalism in East Asia and Asia-Pacific after the Asian crisis', *The Pacific Review* 14(3): 339–72.

Wesley M. (1999) 'The Asian crisis and the adequacy of regional institutions', *Contemporary Southeast Asia* 21: 54–73.

Wolf, M. (2008) *Fixing Global Finance*, Baltimore: The Johns Hopkins University Press.

World Bank (2010) *Emerging Stronger from the Crisis: East Asia and Pacific Economic Update 2010, Vol. 1*, Washington, DC: World Bank.

Xinhua News Agency (2010) 'Chinese President calls for strong, sustainable, balanced global economic growth', 27 June.

Yokoi-Arai, M. (2006) 'Legal and political effects of financial and monetary regional integration in Asia', *Law and Business Review* 12(1): 47–69.

Yoshitomi, M. and Ohno, K. (1999) 'Capital-account crisis and credit contraction: the new nature of crisis requires new policy responses', *Asian Development Bank Institute Working Paper No. 2*. Tokyo, Japan, accessed at http://www.adbi.org/publications/wp/wp9905.htm. [Accessed 25 March 2002].

Zhou, X. (2009) 'Reform the international monetary system', accessed at http://www.bis.org/review/r090402c.pdf (accessed 15 August, 2010).

The future of regional liquidity arrangements in East Asia: lessons from the global financial crisis

William W. Grimes

Abstract The global financial crisis of 2008–09 presented a critical challenge to East Asian regional financial cooperation. Over a decade of efforts to reduce regional vulnerability to financial crisis and contagion were confronted with the worst global economic crisis since the 1930s. The results for East Asia were mixed. On the one hand, no economies were forced to submit to IMF-led bailouts, as had happened so painfully in 1997–98. On the other hand, the most highly-developed component of the project of ASEAN+3 financial regionalism – the Chiang Mai Initiative (CMI), which set up a system of emergency liquidity provision – appeared irrelevant, as the central banks of South Korea and Singapore prioritized the establishment of new swap agreements with the United States as a means of ensuring dollar liquidity instead of relying on their Chiang Mai partners. Nonetheless, in May 2009, the ASEAN+3 finance ministers agreed to a substantial expansion and 'multilateralization' of the initiative. This paper critically addresses whether CMI has been transformed into an 'Asian Monetary Fund' and argues that the events of 2008–10 make substantial additional movement in that direction unlikely.

The Asian Financial Crisis of 1997–98 was an epochal moment for East Asia. More traumatic than memory or geographical distance allow most US and Europe-based observers to realize today, it opened up a 'politics of resentment' (Higgott 1998) that in turn spawned new and unprecedented

---

William W. Grimes is a Professor of International Relations at Boston University. He is the author of *Currency and Contest in East Asia: The Great Power Politics of Financial Regionalism* (Cornell University Press, 2009) and *Unmaking the Japanese Miracle: Macroeconomic Politics, 1985–2000* (Cornell University Press, 2001).

efforts among the East Asian economies to pursue regional solutions to the vulnerabilities created by financial globalization. Starting with the abortive Japanese proposal for an Asian Monetary Fund (AMF) in 1997, financial regionalism has deepened and expanded in the years since the crisis.

While financial regionalism includes a variety of initiatives, the core of the efforts – and by far the most developed of them – has been the Chiang Mai Initiative (CMI). The functional heir to the AMF proposal, the CMI is a mechanism by which ASEAN+3 economies can provide emergency liquidity to their counterparts quickly, in large amounts, and in a coordinated manner in the event of a currency crisis. By 2010, CMI had at least nominally developed into a reserve pooling agreement encompassing all of the governments of the ASEAN+3, with committed funds totaling $120 billion. Although the CMI had not been tested as of June 2011, it constituted a substantial ASEAN+3 commitment to regional stability.

The global financial crisis of 2008–09 presented a potentially critical challenge to East Asian regional financial cooperation. The institutions created over a decade to reduce regional vulnerability to financial crisis and contagion were confronted with the worst global economic crisis since the 1930s. As it turned out, the East Asian economies were spared financial crises or runs on their currencies, and Chiang Mai did not need to be invoked. Nonetheless, the crisis hastened moves by the ASEAN+3 finance ministers to 'multilateralize' and expand the CMI, igniting speculation that CMI would be transformed into a de facto AMF.

This paper analyzes the political and economic implications of CMI multilateralization and expansion. Unlike most analyses to date, it demonstrates that the changes are less dramatic than they appear and by no means constitute an Asian Monetary Fund of the sort envisioned in 1997 by the Japanese Ministry of Finance or in the years since by proponents of regionalism. It also analyzes the daunting challenges to the creation of a purely regional institution in light of the global financial crisis.

To make the case, the paper is organized as follows: the first section will briefly address the rationale and history of the Chiang Mai Initiative and summarize some of the key debates about it. The second section will consider the effects of the global financial crisis on the East Asian economies. The third section will describe in some detail CMI Multilateralization (CMIM) and related changes to which the ASEAN+3 finance ministers agreed in 2009–10. The fourth section will analyze the meaning and effects of those changes in terms of effectiveness, credibility, and moral hazard, making the case that CMIM remains nested within global regimes and is likely to continue to be so. A brief review of the eurozone's sovereign debt problems of 2010–11 further strengthens that case.

Chiang Mai Initiative: origins, development, debates

A variety of authors have written at length about the origins of the Chiang Mai Initiative (Dieter and Higgott 2003; Henning 2002; Amyx 2004;

Calder and Ye 2004; Hayashi 2006; Lee 2006, 2008; Grimes 2006, 2009a; Katada 2004; Chey 2009). While these authors approach CMI from a variety of perspectives, several common threads emerge. The Asian Financial Crisis demonstrated not only the vulnerability of East Asian economies to the vagaries of global finance, but also the inadequacy of existing mechanisms for dealing with large-scale crises in open and fundamentally well-managed economies. The existing facilities of the International Monetary Fund were nowhere near large enough to address the foreign exchange needs of the crisis economies, nor was there an orderly procedure for pooling together more hard currency to lend to them. Moreover, it was widely agreed (at least within the region) that IMF conditionality had been both misguided and excessively harsh, needlessly worsening and prolonging the crisis and contributing to contagion.

Dissatisfaction with the ad hoc manner in which the bail-out funds were negotiated among the IMF, states, and multilateral development banks, as well as unhappiness with the terms of the bail-outs, prompted regional states to seek an institutional means by which to handle future crises better.[1] The Japanese government's AMF proposal was the first manifestation of this desire. It called for a regional fund of about $100 billion that could be disbursed quickly and without onerous conditions. It was opposed by the IMF and the United States due to their concern that it would create moral hazard (and perhaps due also to their concern that it would usurp their monopoly power or hegemony). It was also opposed by China, apparently out of concern that it was a Japanese power grab. Given the uncertainties associated with it, even some of those economies in crisis or most at risk of contagion chose not to support the plan. After the failure of the AMF proposal, the United States proposed the creation of the Manila Framework Group, which did not guarantee provision of funds but did put in place some ideas about surveillance. It limped along in a desultory fashion for a few years and then died a quiet and apparently unlamented death. Japan, meanwhile, unilaterally implemented the New Miyazawa Initiative, making available an announced $30 billion to address the aftermath of the crisis and to prevent future crises.

Finally, in 2000, the ASEAN+3 finance ministers announced the Chiang Mai Initiative. The initiative consisted of a series of bilateral swap agreements (BSAs) between China, Japan, South Korea, and the ASEAN-5. The CMI was configured as a supplement to the IMF, and the bulk of the funds (initially 90%, falling to 80% after 2005) were tied to crisis economies' willingness to submit to IMF conditionality.

The meaning of this 'IMF link' has been an object of contention among observers, many of whom also felt unease about the institutional messiness of the overlapping and non-uniform BSAs. Roughly speaking, the debate can be broken up into three separate camps, based on an analytical approach. Analysts (e.g., Lee 2006, 2008) who looked at regional financial cooperation from the perspective of regional identity saw the CMI as one of a series of steps toward the eventual creation of an AMF that would be autonomous from the IMF and US pressure. They saw the incrementalist approach to its development as a necessary ruse, designed to minimize opposition from those two symbols of Western market fundamentalism. Liberals (e.g., Girardin 2004; Olarn 2004; Kuroda 2005; Kawai 2005, 2010), including many economic policymakers, focused on the need to better develop the institutions for coordinating disbursement of funds and managing effective policy surveillance. These authors saw the problems of moral hazard and credibility as important but surmountable. Other authors (e.g., Narine 2003; Rhee 2004; Grimes 2006, 2009a, 2011) focused more directly on the political difficulties of achieving regional financial cooperation when the leading states were engaged in a contest for regional power. In my own work, I have argued that the IMF link is the only practical way in which moral hazard can be avoided as long as Japan and China are unable or unwilling to exert a cooperative hegemonic leadership.

Effects of the global financial crisis

While authors have a variety of perspectives on the effectiveness and potential of the Chiang Mai Initiative, all agree that CMI was created with the intention of preventing – or at least managing – future financial and currency crises. If the Asian Financial Crisis was, as former Japanese Vice-Minister of Finance for International Affairs Sakakibara Eisuke (1998) put it, a 'crisis of global capitalism', CMI and other aspects of financial regionalism were created to defend East Asian economies in the next crisis. Inevitably, the question arises of how ASEAN+3 financial regionalism has fared in the global financial crisis of 2008–09.

For the most part, East Asia rode out the crisis extremely well. Despite economic challenges created by loss of export demand, there were no serious financial crises or currency crises, and governments responded effectively with fiscal and monetary stimulus plans. That said, it is difficult to say much about whether regional financial cooperation made a serious difference. The resilience of the East Asian economies was largely based on their own previous individual policies, including accumulation of large foreign exchange reserves, conservative fiscal policies that allowed them to implement massive fiscal stimulus programs, and (outside of China) floating exchange rates. The existence of the CMI swap-lines may or may not have contributed to stability, but there appears to be no evidence of such an effect.

Backstopping regional liquidity: the case of Korea

The closest thing there was to a test of CMI was the Korean near-crisis in autumn 2008. In the event, neither CMI nor South Korea's ASEAN+3 partners were really tested. Nonetheless, it has inspired considerable reflection from advocates of regional cooperation (e.g., Kawai 2009, 2010). Many aspects of the Korean situation remain confusing, but the basic narrative is simple enough. Despite accumulated foreign exchange reserves of approximately $200 billion,[2] the Bank of Korea (BOK) became so concerned about dollar liquidity in the banking system that it rapidly negotiated a $30 billion swap agreement with the US Federal Reserve, which was announced on 30 October, Seoul time. (Simultaneously, the Fed announced new swap lines with Singapore, Brazil, and Mexico; a swap agreement with New Zealand was announced the previous day (*Reuters* 2008).)

The decisions by the Korean and Singaporean authorities to ensure their dollar liquidity through agreements with the Fed did not reflect favorably on the utility or credibility of the Chiang Mai Initiative to prevent and address currency crises, a point that has been acknowledged ruefully by Kawai Masahiro, a prominent advocate of regionalism (Kawai 2009: 24). This should not really be surprising; after all, the IMF link means that the bulk of CMI cannot be released until a crisis economy is in negotiations with the IMF. For a sophisticated, globalized, and increasingly open economy like South Korea, the loss of market confidence that would result from going to the IMF would be extremely painful. In recognition of that fact, the central banks of China, Japan, and South Korea had already established small 'peacetime' BSAs in 2005 that operate outside of their formal CMI swap obligations. Although these BSAs are in principle expandable, the BOK did not go first to its regional swap partners, but to the United States. It is true that the peacetime BSAs with Japan and China were expanded to $20 billion and RMB 180 billion (approximately $26 billion) respectively a month and a half after the Fed swap line was agreed. However, those lines were not utilized at all, whereas the BOK drew on the Fed swap line five times in December 2008 and January 2009 for a total of $16.3 billion (BOK n.d.).[3] Although it is not surprising that CMI itself was not a part of the Korean strategy to avoid a currency crisis, it is striking that Korea and Singapore turned first to the United States rather than their ASEAN+3 partners to ensure the stability of their financial systems – all the more so when we recall that the United States had been explicitly excluded from regional financial cooperation because of worries of US dominance.

The decision to turn to the United States rather than to ASEAN+3 partners calls out for explanation. After all, ASEAN+3 financial regionalism was justified by many of its supporters on the basis of protecting East Asian economies from financial globalization on the US model. Part of the explanation is that the Korean banking system required dollar liquidity, while the peacetime BSAs are denominated in local currencies (i.e., yen–won, RMB–won, RMB–yen). Setting aside the question of why the BSAs were designed to provide non-dollar currencies while also frowning on conversion into dollars by the borrower, there are two larger issues to consider about the role of the US dollar in East Asia and indeed the world. First, the dollar was so dominant as an international currency in the region that the BOK perceived a minimal need even for yen (a major international currency, not to mention the currency of one of Korea's largest partners in trade and investment). Second, it speaks to the massive structural power of the dollar and of the United States in the international monetary system that not only Korea but also a host of other important emerging economies chose to establish temporary swap lines with the Fed to prevent speculative attacks on their currencies.[4] Even with US financial markets and financial institutions at their weakest moment in 70 years or more, the Fed and the dollar remained the ultimate guarantor of liquidity and market confidence both globally and in East Asia.

East Asian economies' responses to the crisis

East Asia's emerging economies entered the crisis in sound fiscal condition, with well-capitalized financial institutions and massive foreign exchange reserves. This gave them the wherewithal to engage in massive stimulus plans (Fitch 2009). While China's fiscal and monetary stimulus that began in 2009 gained particular worldwide attention, virtually every East Asian economy responded similarly. And, as elsewhere, macroeconomic authorities made their decisions based on local conditions and expectations of demand rather than in a coordinated manner. Most economies other than China had also long since shifted from pegged to more flexible exchange rates, which (combined with copious reserves) made speculation and one-way bets less likely to be profitable. Thus, unlike in 1997, even major exchange rate adjustments were orderly and did not lead to currency crises. Not surprisingly, the onset of global crisis brought with it significant divergence of exchange rates in the region, despite ongoing but halfhearted discussions about coordination. All in all, East Asia effectively rode out the crisis despite being buffeted by declining demand in developed country markets.

It is hard not to think of the performance of East Asian emerging economies in the midst of the global financial crisis as a triumph of post-Asian financial crisis policies. However, it is important to note that the triumph was of *national* policies rather than regional ones (Grimes 2009b). This is not surprising, insofar as macroeconomic policy coordination is always and everywhere a difficult challenge. But it does serve as a reminder that, despite all the efforts put into regional cooperation to prevent and manage financial crises, ASEAN+3 cooperation played little evident role in 2008–10.

Regionalist responses to the crisis

Although regional arrangements such as CMI were at best peripheral to the course of the crisis in East Asia, ASEAN+3 responded by accelerating efforts to expand and enhance regional cooperation, particularly through CMIM and the establishment of the ASEAN+3 Macroeconomic Research Office (AMRO) to improve surveillance.[5] The agreement on these enhancements in Tashkent on 2 May 2010 appeared in many ways to be a fulfillment of the CMI roadmap that the ASEAN+3 finance ministers had established five years earlier (Ministry of Finance of Japan n.d.).

The agreement standardized country agreements around a single contract superseded the bilateral swap network with a reserve pooling agreement and a weighted voting system for disbursement, and set up a mechanism to improve surveillance (ASEAN+3 2009). To some observers, CMIM and AMRO constituted a major step toward the vision of a regional fund delinked from IMF oversight (Oh 2009). Others have been more measured in their appraisals (Henning 2009; Grimes 2009b, 2011), though still acknowledging that the changes have been significant.

Before addressing the implications of CMIM for regional politics and economic governance, it is important to consider some of the details of what the ASEAN+3 countries agreed to. This seems like an obvious place to start, but it is in reality somewhat difficult because the actual agreement has not been released.[6] We are left with analyzing the official announcements, whose terse, bureaucratic language can also be somewhat slippery, making it easy for observers to choose to emphasize one statement (e.g., 'lending issues will be decided through majority') over another (e.g., that CMIM is intended 'to supplement the existing international financial arrangements').

It should therefore be useful to clarify what the agreement actually does as opposed to what proponents claim it does. The main enhancements of CMIM are:[7]

1. The expansion of the total committed funds from approximately $80 billion to $120 billion.
2. The assignment of specific financial commitments (known as 'contributions', although the funds are not centrally managed) to each participating country, based loosely on economic size. The ASEAN countries together commit 20% of the total, and the +3 countries account for the rest – 32% Japan, 32% China (including 3.5% by Hong Kong), and 16% for Korea.
3. The amount that each country can draw is equivalent to its contribution multiplied by its 'borrowing multiple'. Borrowing multiples range from 0.5 for China and Japan to 1 for South Korea to 2.5 for the ASEAN-5 and Hong Kong to 5 for the remaining ASEAN members (Brunei, Cambodia, Laos, Myanmar, and Vietnam), reflecting the perceived likelihood of a bailout as well as CMI partners' ability to provide one. This means, for example, that Korea can draw up to $19.2 billion while Malaysia and Indonesia can draw up to $11.925 billion in a crisis.
4. Contributions correspond with voting rights, creating a system of weighted voting for disbursement of funds. A majority vote (actually, two-thirds majority, although this number has not been publicized) in favor of disbursement contractually obliges all members to disburse funds proportionate to their contribution percentage, except under specific conditions, such as financial exigency or political barriers to providing

funds to a specific member country. (The latter condition essentially allows democratic governments not to provide aid to a country like Myanmar, which their laws may not allow them to support financially.) Decisions not related to funding will continue to be decided by consensus.
5. Despite characterizations of CMIM as a system of 'reserve pooling', there is no centralized fund. Rather, CMIM 'contributions' are in fact contractual commitments to disburse a portion of nationally-managed foreign exchange reserves under specific circumstances.

Most of the claims that CMIM is equivalent to the AMF hinge upon the establishment of weighted voting for disbursement of funds. The apparent significance of this procedure has been amplified by the decision to enhance surveillance by establishing an independent economic unit (AMRO) and 'improving' (in unspecified ways) the Economic Review and Policy Dialogue (ERPD) process. Functionalist proponents of AMF have been arguing for years that the development of an autonomous surveillance capability will allow ASEAN+3 to finally jettison its dependence on the much-disliked IMF (e.g., Girardin 2004; Olarn 2004; Kawai 2005, 2010). The combination of CMIM and AMRO appears to move that vision much closer to fruition.

Reality is somewhat murkier than it appears, however. First, the underpublicized requirement of a two-thirds majority of the weighted vote gives near-veto power to both Japan and China. Second, despite the creation of a mechanism for weighted voting, the IMF link is still in place and the ASEAN+3 finance ministers have explicitly stated that CMIM is meant to 'supplement the existing international financial arrangements' – in other words, the IMF. Thus, a vote by member countries as to whether or not to disburse funds will only come once the crisis country has entered negotiations with the IMF. In a sense, this makes the disbursal of funds *more* uncertain than it was under the old BSAs since it subjects the full swap amount to a vote, although it seems highly unlikely that members will vote against providing funds to counterparts that have already committed to accept IMF conditionality. Third, there has been no change in the obligation of member countries to provide unlinked funds (i.e., up to 20% of the country's borrowing maximum), which are still provided at the discretion of the lending country.

Another important point is that the CMIM's 'single contractual arrangement' creates obligations not only for potential lenders, but also for potential borrowers. A key condition is the IMF link, which subjects countries to IMF conditionality in order to access funds beyond 20% of their borrowing maximum. There are, moreover, preconditions in place. While these conditions have not been made public, Japanese Ministry of Finance officials state that there is at least a minimal condition that countries maintain sufficient foreign exchange reserves to cover three months-worth of short-term debt repayments and three months-worth of imports. (Similar conditions existed in most of the old BSAs as well, but they were not standardized.)

Finally, it is unclear exactly how AMRO will operate, including what standards it will apply, how its autonomy will be ensured, or even how its analysis will be used in CMIM decisionmaking. The same questions apply to ERPD. I address this issue below.

Limits of regional cooperation

It is easy to understand why AMF proponents, whether coming from the regional identity or liberal perspective, are excited about CMIM. Although it is clear that CMIM is not yet the fulfillment of the AMF dream, it makes a number of steps in that direction. But a series of questions remains.

I begin with the assumption that, whatever the commitment of regional economic policymakers might be to the idea of a common identity or opposition to financial globalization, they will not go fully down the road to an AMF if it cannot be made to work economically and politically. Practically speaking, this means it must work from the perspective of potential lenders (particularly China and Japan), since lenders hold the whiphand in CMI (Grimes 2006; Henning 2009). The rest of this section critically examines the economic and political practicality of the AMF concept as currently advocated by its proponents. Using a combination of rational institutionalist and realist insights, it develops concepts of *ex ante* and *ex post* conditionality to probe potential weaknesses. It also looks at the lessons for East Asia of the Greek crisis of 2010.

Surveillance and the IMF link

Both liberal and realist analysts of East Asian financial regionalism have recognized that the fundamental challenge for creating a truly autonomous AMF is how to simultaneously address the problems of credibility and moral hazard (Kuroda and Kawai 2003; Grimes 2009a; Kawai 2009). Credibility among both potential crisis economies and potential speculative attackers hinges on creating certainty that a bail-out will be provided if a crisis erupts. However, such certainty may also reassure potential crisis countries that they will be bailed out even if it is their own risky behavior that has made them vulnerable to a crisis, leading to a situation of moral hazard. To eliminate the potential moral hazard, lenders must therefore establish credibility that irresponsible states will be punished if they bring a crisis upon themselves. This must be done through the imposition of strict *ex ante* or *ex post* conditionality.

The distinction between *ex ante* and *ex post* conditionality is an important, if underappreciated one. In principle, effective enforcement can be built on either, so it is important to consider both possibilities in assessing the CMIM enforcement regime. What I call *ex ante* conditionality (also known as preconditionality) essentially means a credible threat to turn away requests from a neighbor for emergency funding if it has not fulfilled certain macroeconomic preconditions meant to reduce vulnerability. In the case of CMI and CMIM, this would mean leaving the crisis country to fend for itself or go to the IMF for a conditionality-laden bail-out. *Ex post* conditionality is what the IMF already does – in other words, assessing the situation critically, giving strict assignments to crisis governments, and withholding subsequent tranches of bail-out money if those conditions are not met.

Dissatisfaction over the IMF's *ex post* conditionality in 1997–98 was of course the trigger for the original AMF proposal and its successors. Much of the rhetoric of regionalism advocates has been focused on the need to provide liquidity support quickly and without strict conditions. But implicitly, all these statements have assumed that crisis economies will be innocent victims of hot money. Policymakers have been more conservative with their taxpayers' billions of dollars, however, recognizing the possibility that crises might well be triggered by irresponsible macroeconomic or financial policies.

So far, CMI and CMIM have dealt with the problem of moral hazard by delegating *ex post* conditionality to the IMF (Kawai 2009) through an *ex ante* commitment to link their funding to IMF funding. But AMF advocates clearly reject the blanket use of the IMF link as the basic decisionmaking principle for fund disbursement.

So how can the participants reduce moral hazard? Regional identity-based analysts typically do not address this question, but the institutionalists certainly do (Kuroda and Kawai 2003; Girardin 2004; Olarn 2004; Kawai 2005, 2009, 2010). For them, the answer is clear: an effective surveillance mechanism that will be used to enforce *ex ante* conditionality. If a country were seen to be acting irresponsibly, then it would be warned through AMRO and ERPD; if it did not improve its policies and a crisis ensued, then the CMIM members would not approve funds without *ex post* conditions. Other authors (e.g. Rhee 2004; Grimes 2006, 2009a, 2011) are suspicious that a surveillance regime of this sort can or will be effective. Their objections are based on three assumptions: that surveillance cannot be made apolitical or 'objective' in the context of the ASEAN+3, that potential lenders will not be politically absolved of a decision to impose strict conditions or refuse to provide funds simply because they based their decision on an 'autonomous' surveillance process, and that credibility cannot be maintained on all sides at a lower cost than through the IMF link.

These are difficult objections to overcome. The first two essentially relate to the utility of international organizations as a locus of delegated authority. First, is it possible to make surveillance apolitical and objective in the ASESAN+3 context? Certainly there are international organizations that have achieved such delegated autonomy – indeed, the IMF itself springs to mind (Woods 2006; Barnett and Finnemore 2004). However, the small size of the ASEAN+3 exposes individual member states to high levels of in-group pressure to approve bailouts; therefore, the automatic nature of the IMF link is a necessity to avoid being blamed for forcing a crisis economy to subject itself to the IMF's potentially drastic *ex post* conditionality (Grimes 2009a).

Effective delegated authority could in principle be an alternative decisionmaking mechanism that would reduce such pressures, and indeed many regionalism advocates point to the effectiveness of the EU in enforcing common policies that affect everything from financial regulation to fiscal policies to food labeling to penal codes. Such hopes appear to be premature at best, however. Leaving aside for the moment the Greek crisis, neither the ASEAN+3 nor even the more institutionalized ASEAN bears a strong resemblance to the EU, whose endless layers of bureaucracy and delegated decisionmaking build on decades of treaty-based incremental progress that for most of its existence was carried out among democratic Cold War allies with roughly similar levels of economic development. The EU bureaucratic superstate itself has been effective largely due to a unique mixture of benevolent leadership by leading economies, transfer payments and access to goods and labor markets to buy off the less fortunate, and an elaborate architecture of political commitments and issue linkages. None of these conditions hold in East Asia.

The work of scholarly advocates of regionalism (e.g., Kawai 2009; Takagi 2010) has shaped the ASEAN+3 decision to create multi-track surveillance (consisting of ERPD, AMRO, and regional thinktank networks). Essentially, the new system creates a division of labor in which ideas about how to measure financial stability are to be developed externally (through ASEAN+3 Research Projects, the Network of East Asian Thinktanks, and the Asian Development Bank's Office of Regional Economic Integration), actual economic performance is to be assessed by AMRO, and policy prescriptions and *ex ante* conditionality are to be proposed or imposed through ERPD. This multi-track structure has a certain technocratic appeal, insofar as it separates elements of design and implementation. By creating an agreed set of principles and metrics and then applying them separately on an ongoing basis, the hope is that there will be less scope for political gaming of the system. The parallels to domestic regulation are obvious.[8] Unfortunately, they are also misleading, since international coordination challenges (which, after all, occur in an anarchic state system) are fundamentally different from domestic ones.

The question of whether surveillance can be objective and apolitical hinges on AMRO. Since AMRO has yet to be established, any statement about it is necessarily speculative, but the basics are clear enough – it is to be an independent research and monitoring unit based in Singapore with a small number of eminent regional economists overseeing a full-time staff of perhaps 50 junior economists. The leaders are to be appointed by the ASEAN+3 finance ministers, and those leaders will in turn be responsible for hiring and delegating to staff. The whole idea of AMRO 'independence' hinges on the assumption that economists seconded from ASEAN+3 think-tanks, universities, and governments for such an important function will actually be independent from their home governments. This may not require much of a stretch of the imagination for Japanese or Korean government appointees, but it seems very much of a bridge too far for non-democratic polities such as China, Vietnam, and Laos. Nor should the recently reported tussle between China and Japan over who will lead AMRO (which has, embarrassingly, delayed its formal establishment) give regionalism advocates much confidence in AMRO autonomy (*Associated Press* 2010).

Even if AMRO does not operate completely apolitically, it might be argued, it will still be fairly transparent and will most likely act in the interests of leading CMIM/AMF states and thus be useful. Perhaps. But that brings us to the second objection: that potential lenders will not be able to avoid being blamed for decisions to deny funding or impose conditionality because those decisions cannot effectively be 'laundered' (to use Abbott and Snidal's 1998 term) through the surveillance process. It is hard to imagine that delegation of the surveillance function will be able to provide plausible deniability for member states if the surveillance process is itself politicized.

If we accept the first two objections to the game-changing potential of surveillance, the third becomes unavoidable. Even if surveillance provides useful data and agreed common knowledge, no CMIM/AMF member state can elide responsibility for its vote to disburse or not to disburse funds. In the absence of the IMF link or clear and consistent Chinese–Japanese cooperation and commonality of interests, the pressure to bail out a troubled economy will become too politically costly to fend off, leading us back to the problem of moral hazard. Or, alternatively, to market uncertainty about how and whether the regional mechanism will work. Neither should be acceptable for the leading potential lenders, China and Japan.

Another challenge for the credibility of ASEAN+3 surveillance is the issue of what standards AMRO will use to monitor regional economies. Given East Asian resentment of the IMF's 1997–98 application of standards developed for Latin American economies, it is not surprising that there has been talk for years of designing measures more appropriate to East Asian economic realities (Yoshitomi and Ohno 1999; ADB 2005a, 2005b, 2007). So far, however, efforts to develop alternative standards have not been very successful either on their own terms or with respect to market credibility. There may well be strong institutional pressure to come up with new standards, since otherwise AMRO surveillance would simply mimic what the IMF does, albeit without the IMF's track record or budget. But confusion over standards is not likely to be reassuring to markets or states in the event of a crisis. Indeed, in response to a question about the possibility of just such a scenario, one senior Japanese financial policymaker told me unequivocally in 2009, 'There cannot be two different standards.'

Limits of CMIM as crisis manager

The 2008 Korean near-crisis exposed another limitation of CMI, which has not changed in any meaningful way with CMIM. Although the 1997–98 South Korean crisis provided a major rationale for regional liquidity arrangements, CMI and CMIM are simply not designed to deal with a crisis in Korea. Practically speaking, they are configured to address a currency crisis in an ASEAN-4 country – a worthy goal, but not quite the goal that regionalism advocates have envisaged for ASEAN+3. CMIM itself is set up to deal with severe crises, hence the attention to conditionality (both *ex ante* conditionality and by the IMF *ex post*). CMIM funds may stop a currency crisis in its tracks; if not, they become first bridge financing and then supplement to an IMF program. But for an advanced and highly open economy like South Korea, IMF involvement would lead to massive disruptions in the form of capital flight, loss of trade finance, and domino effects across its increasingly sophisticated financial sector. For the regional process to benefit South Korea, it needs to have a means of providing access to dollars rapidly and without ambiguity of commitment, but such speed and certainty are not inherent in CMI or CMIM.

This limitation has been apparent to policymakers for some time, and indeed concern over it gave rise to the establishment of peacetime BSAs among the central banks of China, Japan, and South Korea in 2005. Although small (totaling $7 billion), they were set up outside the CMI processes to address short-term liquidity needs unrelated to fundamental economic problems. (The BOK's much larger crisis-period swaps with the BOJ and PBOC were temporary, and have expired.) Such central bank agreements have a long history, and have been of great importance in preventing crises and stabilizing global financial flows. Among other advantages, they can be deployed quickly and flexibly. But central banks have also typically been very careful to ensure that swaps are certain to be paid back. For this reason, the peacetime BSAs among China, Japan, and South Korea are not designed to be used in the case of major currency shifts, and are subject to significant *ex ante* conditionality and lender discretion. In 2008, Korea nearly fell into the gap between CMIM and the peacetime BSAs.

In theory, a fully-realized AMF could offer a solution by providing large-scale support without the IMF taint, based on effective *ex ante* conditionality (Kawai 2010). There is, as we have seen, ample reason to be skeptical of the credibility of such an arrangement. But perhaps South Korea and Singapore are subject to so much market-based scrutiny that funding without strict conditions might not be dangerous. I personally would be inclined to accept the proposition that the costs of not immediately bailing out South Korea in a crisis would far outweigh the dangers of moral hazard. But CMIM is an ASEAN+3 mechanism, and where would members draw the line between South Korea and, say, Malaysia? Or Malaysia and Thailand? The ASEAN+3 states have not shown themselves eager to differentiate in this way among members, bringing us back to the problem of imposing either *ex ante* or *ex post* conditionality. In the end, it will probably be better for ASEAN+3 unity to avoid addressing the gap, and instead to rely on *ad hoc* cooperation.

Power and politics

I have thus far focused on issues of institutional design, based on fairly generic political assumptions such as the problems of moral hazard and enforcement in an anarchical system (Abbott and Snidal 1998; Koremenos et al. 2001). But East Asian regionalism is also fundamentally shaped by two political realities. One is Sino-Japanese distrust and rivalry over regional leadership. The second is the global financial hegemony of the United States, which dominates international financial institutions and regimes and whose dollar remains the world's key currency.

The realist political economy literature (Kindleberger 1981; Gilpin 1987; Stein 1990; Grieco 1988; Cohen 2006; Kirshner 1995) has provided a simple answer to the question of how to solve many of the functional cooperation problems presented above: hegemony. If a clear single leader is not available, there is also some hope offered by the European example of cooperative leadership based on an ambitious and profound project of reconciliation by the two leading states. But while Europe may be an inspiration for East Asian regionalism, Chinese–Japanese political condominium is unlikely to be a sound basis for it for years to come, to say the least. This is why advocates of financial regionalism in East Asia have focused their attention on institutional mechanisms to ensure coordinated action. But these institutional mechanisms are unable to resolve what is at its core a political challenge: they cannot simultaneously address all the issues of credibility, effectiveness, and moral hazard in the absence of the IMF link (Grimes 2011).

The second daunting political challenge for East Asian regionalism is the global financial hegemony of the United States. Like it or hate it, the United States is a central player in the financial regionalism drama. Indeed, as any number of authors have argued from various perspectives, East Asian financial regionalism is in many ways a defensive reaction to US power in the financial and monetary realms (Higgott 1998; Sakakibara 2005; Lee 2008; Katada 2008; Grimes 2009a). But all the same, South Korea's near-crisis in 2008 offered a reminder (if one was needed) that East Asia operates on dollars. While not the tight 'East Asian dollar standard' (McKinnon and Schnabl 2004; McKinnon 2005) of the mid-1990s and early 2000s, the dollar dominates in all three basic uses of international money (invoicing, settlement, and foreign exchange reserve holdings) and remains the only meaningful reference currency for exchange rate management. Moreover, despite the loss of status of the US financial and monetary system in the face of the global crisis, the United States remains at the center of global rulemaking and governance of international financial institutions. One way or another, East Asia is inextricably nested within this global system.

Lessons of the eurozone sovereign debt crises[9]

Although Europe had for many years been an inspiration for East Asian regionalism, events in 2010 called into question some of the key assumptions of advocates of ASEAN+3 financial cooperation. The sovereign debt crisis that began in Greece and then spread to other eurozone economies including Ireland, Portugal, Spain, and Italy was not only a historic challenge for the eurozone, but a wake-up call to East Asia. The crises showed the world the difficulties of effective monitoring and *ex ante* enforcement, as well as of creating a bail-out fund that could avoid both moral hazard for weaker economies and resentment on the part of citizens of stronger economies.

A key factor in the Greek crisis was the failure of *ex ante* enforcement. To begin with, surveillance proved to be ineffective. Not only did EU processes miss the extent of the problem, but even the IMF's dire Article IV evaluation of 25 May 2009 underestimated the country's fiscal deficits by around half (IMF 2009). Few analysts would expect that AMRO could do a better job in East Asia. The enforcement mechanism itself also failed. With national central banks unable to devalue or create money, the eurozone was designed to create a hard budget constraint with no means of bailout. It is hard to think of a stricter system of *ex ante* conditionality, but Greece still managed to consistently violate the Growth and Stability Pact, even if we rely on the government's official figures from before the point when the full extent of the problems became known. The Greek crisis was a reminder of the importance of *ex post* conditionality, and in turn the continuing relevance of the IMF in managing crises.

Greece in 2010 presented obvious warning signs for cooperation in East Asia, where there has been far less regional institutionalization, issue linkages, and economic and political convergence than in Europe. But subsequent events were perhaps even more disturbing. In Ireland and Spain, governments that had been fiscally responsible found themselves constrained in their ability to finance the deficits that appeared after the implosion of property bubbles. The Irish government's fateful decision to take over the obligations of the banking system in particular should have brought back old memories for those who were involved in the Asian Financial Crisis. It was another unpleasant reminder that national decisions can easily disrupt collective plans and expectations.

Finally, the response of the eurozone countries as a group was not particularly encouraging from an East Asian point of view. The European Central Bank violated its mandate not to support governments that were having problems funding their operations. The process of negotiating a resolution to the Greek crisis exposed deep rifts among eurozone countries, with German resentment gaining the most headlines. Despite the EU's high level of institutionalization and history of making hard decisions, the IMF was called in partly for liquidity support and partly to devise and enforce *ex post* conditionality. And the new institutional response, in the form of the European Financial Stabilization Mechanism and the European Financial Stabilization Facility, firmly instated the IMF as a participant in making support programs.[10]

Conclusions

The global financial crisis has had profound but contradictory implications for ASEAN+3 financial cooperation and has clearly served as an impetus for significant institutional enhancement and expansion in the form of CMIM and AMRO. The Korean near-crisis in particular appears to have been a significant factor in persuading participants to move forward on those plans.

At the same time, events have also made financial cooperation look less important, or perhaps even counterproductive. East Asian economies emerged from the crisis in a relatively strong position, having avoided financial crises and moved proactively on the fiscal and monetary fronts. But the apparent cohesion was in fact a set of similar yet uncoordinated national policies that had little connection to the substance of regional cooperation. Of greater concern, the eurozone sovereign debt crises laid bare the difficulties of effective surveillance and *ex ante* enforcement even under the best of circumstances. Events in Greece made clear that the problem of moral hazard could not be swept under the rug or assumed away. Moreover, institutional innovation alone could not eliminate the tensions caused by political differences. It is telling in this respect that even the new European Financial Stabilization Facility relies on the IMF for *ex post* enforcement.

Meanwhile, five of the ASEAN+3 economies (China, Indonesia, Japan, Singapore, and South Korea) are playing on the global stage as members of the G20, Financial Stability Board, Basel Committee, and other key institutions. This may make regional cooperation less central to the strategies of the leading East Asian economies, as it gives them an opportunity to venue shop.

It appears likely that CMI Multilateralization and the creation of AMRO will be the last major enhancements to ASEAN+3 liquidity support mechanisms for the time being, at least unless (or until) conditions change significantly – perhaps in the form of the next great financial crisis. Given the risks of moral hazard and uncertainty that would be inherent in a purely regional institution cut loose from the IMF link, this would be a good thing for the region and for the global economy.

Notes

1 The following brief chronology draws mainly on Grimes (2009a) and Lee (2008).
2 Bank of Korea, 'Official Foreign Reserves', Press Release, 3 December 2008. It remains somewhat unclear exactly why BOK officials became so anxious despite having such large reserves, but it appears that those reserves were less liquid than they should have been, because substantial amounts were either invested in illiquid securities or had already been committed to banks through non-transparent transactions.
3 This constituted about 60% of the BOK emergency provision of foreign exchange to domestic financial institutions.
4 Perhaps the best analysis of US structural power in the international monetary and financial systems is Cohen (2006; see also Andrews 2006; Henning 2006; Kirshner 2006).
5 The Asian Bond Markets Initiative was also enhanced through the creation of the $700 million Credit Guarantee and Investment Facility (CGIF). See ASEAN+3, 2010.
6 Indeed, I was told by Japanese Ministry of Finance officials that the text would not be released, so as to reduce the likelihood that speculators would seek to find loopholes to exploit. (This strikes me as a debatable point – to the extent that the key to CMIM's effectiveness will be market credibility, the lack of clarity about who is committed to what and under what circumstances would seem to me to reduce credibility.)
7 The description below draws primarily from the ASEAN+3 Joint Ministerial Statements of 2009 (Bali) and 2010 (Tashkent) as well as extensive discussions with Japanese Ministry of Finance and IMF officials.
8 Given the leading role of the Japanese ministry of Finance in CMI and CMIM, it is perhaps somewhat ironic that the same argument was used to partially break up MOF in 1997, as Mabuchi (1997) demonstrates.
9 This section is necessarily provisional, as a number of key questions remained unresolved as of January 2011. It is based mostly on news reports.
10 On the bright side, the first bond issue of the European Financial Stabilization Facility (EFSF) on 25 January 2011 was wildly successful – with the Japanese government perhaps ironically being the single biggest purchaser (*Bloomberg* 2011). This may not be such a good sign for eurozone stability, however; it is possible that demand for safe EFSF bonds will crowd out purchases of bonds issued by potential crisis economies, compounding their funding problems.

References

Abbott, K. W. and Snidal, D. (1998) 'Why states act through formal international organizations', *Journal of Conflict Resolution* 42(1): 3–32.

Amyx, J. (2004) 'Japan and the evolution of regional financial arrangements in East Asia', in E. Krauss and T. J. Pempel (eds) *Beyond Bilateralism: US–Japan Relations in the New Asia-Pacific* Stanford, CA: Stanford University Press, pp. 198–218.

Andrews, D. (2006) 'Monetary policy coordination and hierarchy', in D. Andrews (ed.) *International Monetary Power*, Ithaca, NY: Cornell University Press, pp. 91–114. ASEAN+3 (2009) 'Joint media statement of the 12th ASEAN Plus Three finance ministers' meeting' http://www.asean.org/22536.htm, accessed 27 June 2011. ASEAN+3 (2010)

'Joint ministerial statement of the 13th ASEAN+3 finance ministers' meeting" http://www.aseansec.org/documents/JMS_13th_AFMM+3.pdf, accessed 27 June 2011.
Asian Development Bank (2005a) *Early Warning Systems for Financial Crises: Applications to East Asia*, New York: Palgrave Macmillan.
Asian Development Bank (2005b) 'Technical assistance: strengthening economic and financial monitoring in selected ASEAN+3 Countries', December (Project number 39579).
Asian Development Bank (2007) 'Enhancing the capacity of selected ASEAN+3 countries for assessing financial vulnerabilities', March (Project number 40565).
Associated Press (2010) 'China, Japan vie for East Asia financial surveillance post', 11 December.
Bank of Korea (n.d.) 'Stabilization of foreign exchange and foreign currency funding markets', accessed at http://www.bok.or.kr/broadcast.action?menuNaviId=1664, 13 August 2010.
Barnett, M. and Finnemore, M. (2004) *Rules for the World: International Organizations in Global Politics*, Ithaca, NY: Cornell University Press.
Bloomberg (2011) 'Japan fuels "overwhelming" $61 billion in orders for EFSF bonds', 25 January.
Calder, K. and Ye, M. (2004) 'Regionalism and critical junctures: explaining the "organization gap" in Northeast Asia', *Journal of East Asian Studies* 4(2): 191–226.
Chey, H. K. (2009) 'The changing political dynamics of East Asian financial cooperation: the Chiang Mai Initiative', *Asian Survey* 49(3): 450–67.
Cohen, B. J. (2006) 'The macrofoundations of monetary power', in D. Andrews (ed.) *International Monetary Power*, Ithaca, NY: Cornell University Press, pp. 31–50.
Dieter, H. and Higgott, R. (2003) 'Exploring alternative theories of economic regionalism: from trade to finance in Asian co-operation?', *Review of International Political Economy* 10(3): 430–55.
Fitch Ratings (2009). 'Bank-support and fiscal measures being implemented in Asia-Pacific', *Asia-Pacific Special Report*, 4 March.
Gilpin, R. (1987) *The Political Economy of International Relations*, Princeton, NJ: Princeton University Press.
Girardin, E. (2004) 'Information exchange, surveillance systems, and regional institutions in East Asia', in Asian Development Bank (ed.) *Monetary and Financial Integration in East Asia: The Way Ahead, Vol.* 1, New York: Palgrave Macmillan, pp. 53–96.
Grieco, J. (1988) 'Anarchy and the limits of cooperation: a realist critique of the newest liberal institutionalism', *International Organization* 42(3): 485–507.
Grimes, W. W. (2006) 'East Asian financial regionalism in support of the global financial architecture? The political economy of regional nesting', *Journal of East Asian Studies*, 6(3): 353–80.
Grimes, W. W. (2009a) *Currency and Contest in East Asia: The Great Power Politics of Financial Regionalism*, Ithaca, NY: Cornell University Press.
Grimes, W. W. (2009b) 'The global financial crisis and East Asia: testing the regional financial architecture', *EAI Fellows Working Paper Series*, no. 20.
Grimes, W. W. (2011) 'The Asian Monetary Fund reborn? Implications of Chiang Mai Initiative Multilateralization', *Asia Policy* 11: 79–104.
Hayashi, S. (2006) *Japan and East Asian Monetary Regionalism: Towards a Proactive Leadership Role*, New York: Routledge.

Henning, C. R. (2002) *East Asian Financial Cooperation*, Washington, DC: Institute for International Economics.

Henning, C. R. (2006) 'The exchange-rate weapon and macroeconomic conflict', in D. Andrews (ed.) *International Monetary Power*, Ithaca, NY: Cornell University Press, pp. 117–38.

Henning, C. R. (2009) 'The future of the Chiang Mai Initiative: an Asian Monetary Fund?', Washington, DC: Peterson Institute for International Economics, Policy Brief PB09-5 (February).

Higgott, R. (1998) 'The Asian economic crisis: a study in the politics of resentment', *New Political Economy* 3(3): 333–56.

International Monetary Fund (IMF) (2009) *Greece: 2009 Article IV Consultation – Staff Report; Staff Supplement; Public Information Notice on the Executive Board Discussion; and Statement by the Executive Director for Greece* (August).

Katada, S. (2004) 'Japan's counterweight strategy: U.S.–Japan cooperation and competition in international finance', in E. Krauss and T. J. Pempel (eds) *Beyond Bilateralism: U.S.–Japan Relations in the New Asia-Pacific*, Stanford, CA: Stanford University Press, pp. 176–97.

Katada, S. (2008) 'From a supporter to a challenger? Japan's currency leadership in dollar-dominated East Asia', *Review of International Political Economy* 15(3): 399–417.

Kawai, M. (2005) 'East Asian economic regionalism: progress and challenges', *Journal of Asian Economics* 16: 29–55.

Kawai, M. (2009) 'Reform of the international financial architecture: an Asian perspective', *ADBI Working Paper*, no. 167 (November).

Kawai, M. (2010) 'From the Chiang Mai Initiative to an Asian Monetary Fund', paper presented at the Columbia University-ADB-ADBI conference on the 'Future Global Reserve System', Tokyo, 17–18 March.

Kindleberger, C. P. (1981) 'Dominance and leadership in the international economy: exploitation, public goods, and free rides', *International Studies Quarterly* 25(2): 242–54.

Kirshner, J. (1995) *Currency and Coercion: The Political Economy of International Monetary Power*, Princeton, NJ: Princeton University Press.

Kirshner, J. (2006) 'Currency and coercion in the twenty-first century', in D. Andrews (ed.) *International Monetary Power*, Ithaca, NY: Cornell University Press, pp. 139–61.

Koremenos, B., Lipson, C. and Snidal, D. (2001) 'The rational design of international institutions', *International Organization* 55(4): 761–99.

Kuroda, H. (2005) *Tsuka no kobo: En, doru, yuro, jinmingen no yukue* [*The Rise and Fall of Currencies: The Fate of the Yen, Dollar, Euro, and Renminbi*], Tokyo: Chuo Koronsha.

Kuroda, H. and Kawai, M. (2003) 'Strengthening regional financial cooperation in East Asia', *PRI Discussion Paper Series* (Ministry of Finance of Japan), no. 03A-10.

Lee, Y. W. (2006) 'Japan and the Asian Monetary Fund: an identity–intention approach', *International Studies Quarterly* 50(2): 339–66.

Lee, Y. W. (2008) *The Japanese Challenge to the American Neoliberal World Order*, Stanford, CA: Stanford University Press.

Mabuchi, M. (1997) *Okurasho wa naze oitsumerareta no ka?* [*Why Is the Ministry of Finance on the Run?*], Tokyo: Chuo Koronsha.

McKinnon, R. I. (2005) *Exchange Rates under the East Asian Dollar Standard*, Cambridge, MA: MIT Press.

McKinnon, R. I. and Schnabl, G. (2004) 'The East Asian dollar standard, fear of floating, and original sin', *Review of Development Economics* 8(3): 331–60.

Ministry of Finance of Japan (n.d.) 'Enhancement of Chiang Mai Initiative (CMI) – 2nd stage' (briefing paper, received by author in May 2005).

Narine, S. (2003) 'The idea of an "Asian Monetary Fund": the problems of financial institutionalism in the Asia-Pacific', *Asian Perspective* 27(2): 65–103.

Oh, Y.H. (2009) 'Asian monetary fund is on the horizon', *Korea Herald*, 25 May.

Olarn, C. (2004) 'Reserve pooling in East Asia: beyond the Chiang Mai Initiative', in Asian Development Bank (ed.) *Monetary and Financial Integration in East Asia: The Way Ahead, Vol. 1*, New York: Palgrave Macmillan, pp. 97–142.

Reuters (2008) 'U.S. Fed launches four new currency swap lines', 29 October.

Rhee, Y. S. (2004) 'East Asian monetary integration: destined to fail?', *Social Science Japan Journal* 7(1): 83–102.

Sakakibara, E. (1998) *Kokusai kin'yu no genba: Shihonshugi no kiki o koete* [*The Arena of International Finance: Moving Beyond the Crisis of Capitalism*], Tokyo: PHP Shinsho.

Sakakibara, E. (2005) *Keizai no sekai seiryokuzu* [*Map of World Economic Power*], Tokyo: Bungei Shunjû.

Stein, A. A. (1990) *Why Nations Cooperate: Circumstance and Choice in International Relations*, Ithaca, NY: Cornell University Press.

Takagi, S. (2010) 'Regional surveillance for East Asia: how can it be designed to complement global surveillance?', *ADB Working Paper Series on Regional Integration*, 50.

Woods, N. (2006) *The Globalizers: The IMF, the World Bank and Their Borrowers*, Ithaca, NY: Cornell University Press.

Yoshitomi, M. and Ohno, K. (1999) 'Capital-account crisis and credit contraction', *ADB Institute Working Paper*, no. 2.

Global economic crisis: boon or bust for East Asian trade integration?

Mireya Solís

Abstract Political economists have long noted that the prospects for trade liberalization diminish in a climate of economic recession. A stagnant economy intensifies the burden of adjustment for non-competitive sectors and polarizes domestic trade politics. Not surprisingly, the global financial crisis has raised concerns of a substantial protectionist backlash, through the imposition of national measures that circumvent WTO disciplines such as anti-dumping or tied stimulus packages. The impact of economic crisis on regional integration is, however, more ambiguous and has not been explored systematically. On the one hand, policymakers may be pressed to renege on trade liberalization commitments on all fronts – also weakening the momentum to negotiate or implement free trade agreements (FTAs). On the other hand, policymakers may be tempted to 'insulate' their region from adverse global trends and may see FTAs as more amenable to political manipulation that shelters inefficient sectors. In order to shed light on the connection between external crisis and regionalist drive, this article assesses three main challenges East Asian elites confront in devising a regional trade bloc capable of acting as a growth locomotive: institutional fit, multilateralization, and architectural design. The track record of East Asian governments of negotiating FTAs to score diplomatic points abroad and ensure political survival at home – at the expense of maximizing economic gains through far-reaching liberalization – does not bode well for the magnitude of this challenge.

Dr. Mireya Solís (Harvard PhD, 1998) is Associate Professor at the School of International Service of American University. She authored *Banking on Multinationals: Public Credit and the Export of Japanese Sunset Industries* (Stanford University Press, 2004), and is co-editor of *Cross-Regional Trade Agreements: Understanding Fragmented Regionalism in East Asia* (Springer, 2008), and *Competitive Regionalism: Explaining the Diffusion and Implications of FTAs in the Pacific Rim* (Palgrave-Macmillan, 2009).

Introduction

Political economists have long noted that the prospects for trade liberalization diminish in a climate of economic recession. A stagnant economy intensifies the burden of adjustment for non-competitive sectors and polarizes domestic trade politics. Not surprisingly, the global economic crisis has raised concern of a substantial protectionist backlash, through the imposition of national measures that circumvent WTO disciplines such as anti-dumping or tied stimulus packages. The impact of economic crisis on regional integration is, however, more ambiguous and has not been explored systematically. On the one hand, policymakers may be pressed to renege on trade liberalization commitments on all fronts – also weakening the momentum to negotiate or implement free trade agreements (FTAs). On the other hand, policymakers may be tempted to 'insulate' their region from adverse global trends and may see FTAs as more amenable to political manipulation that shelters inefficient sectors.

In order to shed light on this issue, this article explores whether the global economic crisis is likely to help or hinder trade integration in East Asia. A very important debate has emerged as to whether East Asia needs to rethink its developmental strategy to ameliorate global imbalances. A key pillar of such policy prescription for 'rebalancing growth' is the development of a region-wide trade bloc. The article assesses the chances that regional integration can emerge rejuvenated from the crisis and that it can play the key role of spurring economic growth. The analysis unfolds in three parts. First, the article surveys the theoretical literature on the impact of economic crisis on trade liberalization, and factors in how forum-shopping (i.e., the existence of alternative venues for trade negotiation) might increase the relative attractiveness of FTAs. Second, the article offers a panorama of FTA proliferation in East Asia to date, since the construction of a region-wide FTA will not begin from a clean slate but must take into account these 'initial conditions'. Third, the article discusses three sets of specific challenges (institutional fit, multilateralization, and architectural design) that must be overcome for a vibrant trade bloc to emerge.

As a preview of the conclusions, the article finds a disconnect between the growing political space that regional elites will most likely enjoy to launch broader integration initiatives (due to the perceived vulnerability of the region), and their inability to negotiate trade agreements that can truly deliver far-reaching liberalization. The past track record is eloquent in showing that East Asian governments have mostly negotiated trade agreements of limited scope as they aim to score political points in their regional diplomacy without confronting the domestic vested interests that oppose deeper economic integration.

1. Economic crisis and regional integration incentives

The divisive politics of trade adjustment has been a mainstay topic in the field of international political economy (Milner 1999). Market liberalization creates winners and losers as internationally competitive manufacturers (those that specialize in relatively abundant factors of production according to standard comparative advantage law) thrive with expanded business opportunities; whereas inefficient producers are beleaguered by the surge of inexpensive imports. Pro- and anti-trade coalitions will form depending on the expected impact of liberalization on their income, and most debate in the literature has centered on whether these trade coalitions will emerge along class cleavages (when there is high factor mobility) or sectoral lines (when low factor mobility causes the interests of labor and capital tied to specific industries to converge) (Rogowski 1989; Alt and Gilligan 1994; Hiscox 2003).[1]

Notwithstanding these debates, a solid consensus exists in the literature that economic downturns polarize trade politics. An adverse macroeconomic climate with growing unemployment magnifies the adjustment burden for non-competitive economic actors and makes them more vocal in their opposition to free trade (Tackacs 1981; Bhagwatti 1988). Brawley (2006) has offered one of the most sophisticated analyses of how macroeconomic conditions influence microeconomic preferences on trade liberalization. He points out that the preferences of some economic actors (scarce factors that are mobile across sectors) are *ambiguous* (not fixed – as depicted in the conventional models discussed above), and these actors operate as a swing group on trade policy. To the extent that a high unemployment rate erodes their mobility across economic sectors, these floating interest groups will come out in favor of protection. A recessionary climate, therefore, tilts the balance towards economic closure.

Nevertheless, the straightforward prediction that recession hinders the chances of trade liberalization is harder to sustain when we take into account the growing complexity of international trade governance that the rapid pace of FTA proliferation has brought about. Conforming to the larger trend of intensified international regime density, the multiplicity of trade forums has altered trade politics in that economic actors can now lobby or government officials can now strategize over *venue selection* to pursue their trade negotiation and adjudication goals (Pekkanen et al. 2007; Busch 2007; Davis 2009). It is therefore conceivable that the impact of an economic crisis is not homogeneous across all trade forums, and that hard economic times may in fact *increase* the relative attractiveness of bilateral or regional negotiations. Indeed, policymakers may be tempted to 'insulate' their region from adverse global trends and/or they may see FTAs as more amenable to political manipulation that shelters inefficient sectors.

Historical precedent suggests that regionalism may thrive during economic downturns. For instance, Mansfield and Milner (1999: 597) locate the second wave of regionalism during the depression years of the interwar period when bilateral agreements were often used to artificially balance commodity trade and/or gain political influence (Condliffe 1940). And the literature on the political economy of FTAs advances several arguments as to why FTAs may appear as a more attractive policy tool during uncertain economic times.

Free trade agreements may offer firms that are competitive at the regional (but not the global level) the chance to achieve economies of scale, thereby creating new job and export opportunities at a time when they are sorely needed (Milner 1997; Chase 2003). On the other hand, Grossman and Helpman (1995) focus on the impact of the domestic political marketplace on the nature of FTAs that can win internal ratification. They reach the conclusion that the 'winning agreements' offer both export and import protectionism by assuring exporters access to higher priced regional markets and keeping competitors at bay, and by protecting sensitive sectors. This dual protectionism is particularly attractive during economic downturns. Bhagwati (2008) emphasizes how the multilateral system is in fact permissive of these trade-diverting FTAs since the WTO (through article 24 rules for industrialized nations and the enabling clause for developing countries) has failed to prevent the proliferation of low quality trade agreements. Pekkanen et al. (2007) bridge the level of analysis between domestic politics and international forums by pointing out the gains/control tradeoff that trade regimes present to policymakers. The multilateral regime (with the largest number of parties and a set of common rules) has the greatest potential to maximize gains from trade, but industrialized nations do not control negotiation outcomes due to high preference heterogeneity among a large membership and coalition tactics by developing nations. In contrast, in bilateral trade agreements with developing nations, industrialized nations open one small market at a time, but they have more leverage over the negotiation agenda as the party with the largest market facing a lower cost of no agreement.[2] Industrialized nations will gravitate towards FTAs because they allow governments to navigate increasingly polarized trade demands at home (as the costs of trade adjustment increase in a recession) by carving niches of preferential market access abroad for its exporters while keeping non-competitive sectors protected.

While the theoretical debate has not settled the question as to whether an economic crisis diminishes the chances of trade opening across all potential venues or makes preferential trade agreements more politically palatable, the empirical record on the ongoing global crisis provides mixed signals as well. On the one hand, there is widespread concern with the rise of creeping or WTO-legal protectionism (Baldwin and Evenett 2009). An early assessment in the spring of 2009 on the spread of protectionist measures found 47 trade-restricting measures imposed by 17 members of the G20 (Gamberoni and Newsfarmer 2009). Taking stock of trade developments in the first year of the global economic crisis, the WTO (2009) recounted several cases of slippage, mostly in the form of reverting to higher bound tariffs (instead of the lower applied tariffs), stimulus packages with 'buy national' conditions, and increasing use of anti-dumping, countervailing duties, and safeguard procedures. For instance, there was a 28% increase in anti-dumping initiations in 2009 compared to 2007, a 115% in countervailing duty queries in the third quarter of 2009 compared to the same period a year earlier, and the second highest peak in safeguard initiations in 2009 with 26 such cases (WTO 2009: 25, 29). The WTO estimated the impact of these trade-restricting measures on world trade flow so far to be modest, at approximately 1% of world merchandise trade.

The moderate protectionist response given the magnitude of the economic downturn is attributed to three main factors: the WTO's institutional safeguards, the spread of global supply chains which makes countries reluctant to impose tariffs that could backfire, and the reliance on expansionary macroeconomic policy to stimulate national economies (Bussiere et al. 2009: 17). While a repeat of the 1930s beggar-thy-neighbor policies of large-scale retaliatory tariffs or competitive currency devaluations does not seem likely, there is nevertheless worry that a new wave of protectionism can stave off any incipient economic growth. As Erixon and Sally (2009: 30) point out, 'the threat comes not from the spiraling protectionism of the 1930s, but the creeping variety of the 1970s'. Intensified use of non-tariff barriers, the lack of clear exit strategies from direct government intervention in the form of bailout packages (the auto sector stands out with $48 billion in subsidies awarded worldwide) with the consequent potential for politicization of economic decisions, and the possibility of growing friction among countries with current account deficits (United States) and surpluses (China), are all reasons for concern (Ahearn 2009; Dadush 2009).[3]

Finally, the decreased support for free trade among the public of industrialized nations has concerned some. The share of Americans and Europeans with a positive view of international trade in a Pew Global Attitudes survey went down in just five years from 80% to 60% in the United States, and from 90% to 80% in the European Union between 2002 and 2007) (Bussiere et al. 2009: 15). This decrease in public support took place *prior* to the crisis and it is likely to drop further with the ongoing recession in the United States and Europe. For instance, maneuvering in the midst of a grueling recession and a jobless recovery, President Obama behaved as a 'passive free trader' in that he will preempt any major protectionist measure but has put on the backburner the trade agenda both for the Doha Round and the string of FTAs awaiting ratification (van Grasstek 2009).

On the other hand, the global economic crisis does not so far seem to have affected the pace of FTA proliferation. Figure 1 shows the number of FTAs by year of notification to the WTO. Although it is too soon to discern long-term trends, a sudden halt to the FTA bandwagon is not apparent. In the years 2008 and 2009, 28 and 20 FTAs respectively were notified. Moreover, the WTO Secretariat (2009: 6) estimates that there are around 100 FTAs currently under negotiation, and as these trade agreements enter into force a rapid rate of FTA proliferation is likely. In fact, East Asian policymakers have voiced their support for ongoing regional integration crisis during hard economic times. Singapore's Foreign

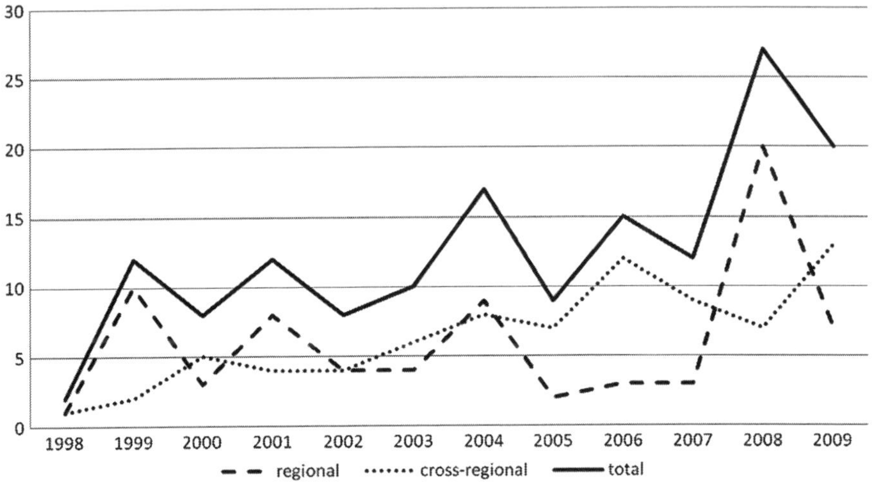

Figure 1 FTA proliferation. Number of FTAs by year of notification to the WTO. Source: WTO database on regional trade agreements.

Minister George Yeo predicted a stronger momentum towards regional integration, just as 'during the Asian financial crisis, some commentators thought ASEAN would be weakened, but the opposite happened. Leaders met and acted decisively, and we became stronger as a regional organization' (*China View* 2009). And at the 2009 APEC meeting convened under the slogan 'sustaining growth, connecting the region', the leaders' declaration put regional integration at the forefront of the recovery agenda: 'We will take a comprehensive approach to build a 21st century model of economic integration that will combine trade liberalisation "*at the border*", improve the business environment "*behind the border*", and enhance supply chain connectivity "*across the border*"' (http://www.apec.org/apec/leaders_declarations/2009/aelm_growthparadigm.html).

But perhaps more significant than these official public statements on the benefits of free trade and regional integration are survey findings that show that East Asian elites tilt heavily in favor of bilateral and regional agreements (and are skeptical about the effectiveness of the WTO) to advance the trade agenda and reactivate their economies (Gill et al. 2009: 16). The weighted responses of elites in nine countries (United States, Australia, China, India, Indonesia, Singapore, Thailand, Japan and South Korea) ranked bilateral FTAs, the WTO, ASEAN+3, and APEC in descending order of effectiveness. There were important variations by country, though. While Thailand and Singapore leaned more towards the WTO and regional agreements over the bilaterals, elites in the United States, Japan, and Korea (with by far the largest degree of support) identified first the bilateral trade agreements as effective venues to promote trade. In terms of the plurilaterals, the United States supported the FTAA and APEC, Japan the ASEAN+6, and Korea the ASEAN+3. Interestingly, Japan and Korea both had the lowest levels of confidence in the WTO (Gill et al. 2009: 16).

These misgivings about the efficacy of the multilateral system raise the question as to whether, following past precedent, this period of severe economic crisis will provide a second wind to the movement for regional integration in East Asia. Indeed, the 1997 Asian Financial Crisis (AFC) is widely credited with enabling significant policy initiatives to decrease financial vulnerability and with propelling the first wave of East Asian regionalism (Macintyre et al. 2008; Bowles 2002; Munakata 2006). Many East Asian governments made great strides in the aftermath of the AFC towards ameliorating the sources of financial vulnerability by amassing foreign exchange reserves, strengthening the prudential regulation of the banking sectors, introducing corporate governance reforms and allowing for greater foreign exchange rate flexibility (MacIntyre et al. 2008: 12–15). Equally important was the shift towards regionalism both in the area of financial cooperation through the Chiang-Mai currency swap agreement and efforts to develop regional bond markets; as well as the negotiation of the first string of preferential trade agreements in the region. Disappointment with American policies during the 1997 crisis and a growing sense of common regional vulnerabilities spurred the movement towards East Asian integration. As dissatisfaction with US leadership and regional weakness converge once more, can we expect East Asian defensive regionalism to reach new depths?

2. Global crisis and a new growth paradigm for East Asia: is regional integration a solution?

Impact of the global economic crisis on East Asia

The burst of the US subprime mortgage market in December 2007, and especially the collapse of the firm Lehman Brothers in September 2008, not only exposed the severe vulnerabilities of the American financial sector where lax regulation had allowed corporations to develop and trade 'toxic assets', but also reflected deep economic interdependence; it produced the worst world depression since the 1930s. Worldwide, the sharp contraction of financial flows, the drop in equity values, the drying up of trade finance, the reduction in corporate investment, and growing unemployment produced a dramatic economic slowdown. Globally, the IMF estimated a decline of world GDP of 1.1% (in purchasing power terms) for 2009, and a contraction of world trade by almost 12% (IMF 2009a).

Surprisingly enough, Asia was seriously affected by the crisis. Even though the financial troubles had clearly started elsewhere, and the banking systems in the region were deemed sound, with a minimal exposure to subprime assets, the contraction of East Asian economies at the onset of the crisis was severe. For instance, emerging East Asia (ASEAN-4, Newly

Industrializing Economies (NIEs), Vietnam, and China) went from a 10.3% GDP growth rate in the second quarter of 2007 to 1.8% in the first quarter of 2009. For China, the drop in GDP growth rate during this period was indeed steep (from 14% to 6.2%), but ASEAN-4 and NIEs actually registered negative GDP growth rates at the trough of the recession in the first quarter of 2009 (−0.4% and −6.2%, respectively) (ADB 2010: 4). And the collapse in exports was also dramatic for several countries. For instance, in the last quarter of 2008 the year-on-year percentage change was −24.6% for Taiwan, −22.3% for Philippines, −12.9% for Singapore, −12.6% for Malaysia, −10.2% for Thailand, and −8.1% for Japan (Athukorala and Kohpaiboon 2009).

These figures underscore the fact that trade was a main mechanism of crisis contagion in Asia.[4] The severity of the blow was particularly shocking because it contravened the conventional wisdom in many Asian policy circles about 'decoupling'. In this view, East Asian countries were increasingly detached from extra-regional markets and the region was evolving into a self-contained area animated by its own economic dynamism. The decoupling thesis rested on three premises: trade linkages with Western industrialized nations (especially the United States) had decreased in importance; China was poised to rise as a regional engine of growth increasingly consuming goods manufactured in the region; and the accumulation of massive foreign reserves significantly diminished the vulnerability of the region to negative external shocks (Pula and Peltonen 2009: 7–8). And this thesis found empirical corroboration in the growing shares of intra-regional trade, which increased from 31% in 1990 to 41% in 2007, and the consequent decline in the share of Asian exports to the United States from 22% to 15% in that period (Kim et al. 2009).

The economic contraction of 2008–2009 revealed the shortcomings of the decoupling argument, however. The main weakness of the trade figures mentioned above is that they do not take into account the expansion of production networks in the region and the widespread prevalence of component trade. Standard intra-regional trade figures are inflated as different components cross borders multiple times, but extra-regional markets continue to be the main destination for final good exports. A number of empirical studies have found no evidence of decoupling, and instead they speak of increasing 'recoupling' in the aftermath of the Asian financial crisis. Using an input–output table, Pula and Peltonen (2009: 21) found that domestic demand made a smaller contribution to value added in Asian countries: from 72.3% in 1995 to 64.3% in 2006, while the increase in the share of intra-regional trade was modest (from 9.2% to 10%). In fact, exports to extra-regional markets were a larger contributor to value added: from 17.2% to 26.6%. Athukorala and Kohpaiboon (2009: 5, 10) show that parts and components play a larger role in overall East Asian exports (26.9%) than in other regions of the world (22.3%); and that the intra-regional share of East Asia's exports of final goods has in fact *decreased* over time from

46% in 1994/95 to 36.9% in 2006/07. In other words, East Asia's regional integration has in fact been fueled by global integration with no real insulation from extra-regional trade shocks.

The 'rebalancing growth' mantra and the role of regional integration

This realization has fueled a vigorous debate in the region regarding structural changes needed to ameliorate this vulnerability. To be sure, thanks to short-term emergency measures such as monetary easing and fiscal spending, East Asian countries engineered a V-shaped recovery, with emerging Asia registering a 10.8% GDP growth rate in the first quarter of 2010, and China's growth was the most spectacular at 11.9% (ADB 2010: 4). Domestic demand – but mostly fixed investment from government stimulus packages and less so internal consumption – is responsible for this remarkable comeback. In the first quarter of 2010, the largest contributors to GDP growth were fixed investment (6%), consumption (3.7%), and net exports (0.2%) in the Asian NIEs. The respective figures for ASEAN-4 were 5.9%, 3.0%, and –0.7% (ADB 2010: 7). And in the case of China, the official stimulus package accounted for 90% of growth in 2009, and consumption merely 10% (Stratfor 2010). Due to relatively robust fiscal balances, many East Asian countries were able to jumpstart their economies through sizable counter-cyclical spending packages (on average representing 7.1% of GDP) (Ahn 2010). Once more, China stood out with a $586 billion stimulus program, equivalent to 14% of GDP.

And yet, as East Asian countries start to unwind their stimulus packages in order to avoid speculative bubbles and restore fiscal balance, the need to correct over-reliance on export growth is all the more pressing. This is imperative given the prognosis for weak demand in advanced industrialized nations. Global imbalances (with the United States running large trade deficits and borrowing heavily from abroad and East Asian countries aggressively targeting exports and accumulating large foreign exchange reserves) are, therefore, at the center of the ongoing debate on Asia's long-term recovery. While global imbalances are not considered in regional policy circles the *cause* of the Asian recession, they are deemed a source of a major *vulnerability* that needs to be corrected by the adoption of a new development paradigm.[5] Hence, the calls for 'rebalancing' growth have multiplied. In essence, the new model emphasizes domestic and regional demand to countervail the excessive reliance on extra-regional markets (Kawai 2009; ADB 2009).

Regarding domestic sources of growth, the policy prescriptions include promoting domestic consumption by developing an extensive social safety net that eliminates the need for precautionary savings; nurturing small and medium sized enterprises (SMEs) that can manufacture goods attuned to domestic needs, and promoting competition especially in the financial sector in order to redirect savings away from foreign bonds into domestic investment opportunities (ADB 2009: 14; Lord 2009: 23). On the other hand, advocates of rebalancing Asia's development paradigm recommend the promotion of region-wide integration through the negotiation of an FTA in order to boost intra-regional trade by facilitating economies of scale, intra-industry trade, and in that way to reduce the over-reliance on advanced country markets (ADB 2009, Kawai 2009). The question then arises whether it is feasible to construct a regional trade bloc capable of operating as the second pillar in the new growth paradigm for the region.

Point of departure: an 'FTA map' of East Asia

To answer this question it is necessary first of all to understand what the current state of play is in Asian regional integration since initial conditions will loom large in the construction of a trade bloc that can energize the region's growth. In glancing at an 'FTA map' of East Asia at least four main traits stand out.

Accelerated FTA proliferation in the 2000s

As can be appreciated from Figure 2, the FTA trend in East Asia is for the most part a twenty-first century phenomenon. Although ASEAN nations had negotiated an FTA in 1992, the multiple lists of exemptions and extended liberalization calendars prevented AFTA from significantly advancing integration in Southeast Asia. In fact, the rates of preference utilization in AFTA have been very low: around 3% in the late 1990s (Baldwin 2007:

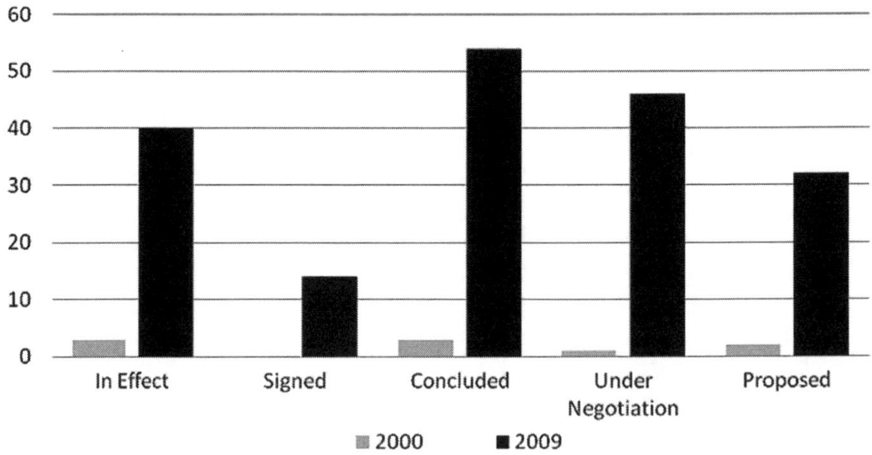

Figure 2 FTA frenzy in East Asia. Source: Based on data available in Kawai and Wignaraja (2009).

12). Instead, market-led integration had prevailed as Japanese companies in the aftermath of the 1985 yen appreciation invested heavily in the region, Southeast Asian nations unilaterally liberalized their economies to attract investment, and China deepened its market reforms in order to become a major assembly export platform (Solís 2004; Baldwin 2007).

In the late 1990s, East Asian countries that hitherto had endorsed exclusive support for the GATT/WTO in trade negotiations began to consider the possibility of developing multi-track trade strategies with the inclusion of preferential trade agreements. This reassessment was influenced not only by the Asian financial crisis which encouraged a search for regional solutions (as discussed above), but was affected by two major developments in the world trading system. First, the stagnation of the WTO with the fiasco of Seattle and later on the protracted negotiations of the Doha Round created the incentive to sign FTAs as an insurance mechanism. Second, the proliferation of FTAs elsewhere in the world put strong competitive pressure on East Asian countries to follow suit. East Asian countries developed FTA strategies to match the actions of their peers and achieve a number of economic (nullifying the trade diversion from prior FTAs, delivering preferential market access to exporters and MNCs, etc.), political (acquiring greater status as an FTA hub, engaging in regional leadership contests, etc.), and rule-making goals (disseminating from the bottom up favorable trade and investment rules) (Solís and Katada 2009).

Fueled by skepticism about the effectiveness of multilateral economic organizations and the blazing regional competition via preferential trade agreements, East Asian countries have launched multiple FTA negotiations. In the short span of a decade, more than 54 FTAs have been concluded (40 of which are in effect, and 14 have been signed). There are currently 46 FTAs under negotiation, and 32 more have been proposed (Kawai and Wignaraja 2009). The FTA wave in East Asia shows no sign of abating.

Bilateralism, not regionalism

The large number of FTAs accumulated in East Asia in a small number of years is in part due to the predominance of bilateral accords instead of broader minilateral or regional agreements. As Table 1 indicates, 74% of all FTA initiatives are bilaterals, while larger groupings are much more infrequent (26%). Moreover, most of these bilateral FTAs are with small trading partners, as can be appreciated in Table 2, which provides a snapshot of FTA strategies of main East Asian countries. In other words, the FTA policy departure has been in many instances a low-risk undertaking targeting small markets unlikely to produce adverse adjustments at home (but also forgoing large gains from trade).

A number of key bilaterals are also missing from this picture: those that would tie the largest Northeast Asian economies (or a trilateral China–Japan–Korea agreement). China first floated the idea of such

Table 1 Characteristics of East Asian FTAs

FTAs by status	No. of FTAs	By configuration		By geographic orientation	
		Bilateral	Plurilateral	Intra-East Asia	Extra-East Asia
Concluded	37	28	9	13	24
Under negotiation	40	30	10	4	36
Proposed	26	18	8	4	22
Total	103	76	27	21	82

Source: Based on data in Kawai and Wignaraja (2009).

trilateral in 2002, but it found a cold reception as both Korea and Japan are wary of the major adjustment in agricultural markets that this would entail (Urata and Pempel 2006). The most progress to date on this initiative is a trilateral feasibility study to be finished by 2012. In the case of Japan, concern from agriculture and labor-intensive manufacturing sectors coupled with a spate of bilateral diplomatic frictions during the Koizumi administration (2001–2006) have prevented so far the negotiation of an FTA with China, despite the strong support for such an agreement from Japan's internationalized business sector (Solís 2009). The official Japanese line has therefore been that China must first show good compliance with its WTO commitments before an FTA can be considered. And although Japan and Korea launched negotiations of a bilateral FTA in 2003, they reached a standstill a year later over Japan's reluctance to open its primary sectors (especially fisheries) and Korea's concern with a ballooning trade deficit and the adjustment burden for SMEs (Katada and Solís 2010). The lack of traction for Northeast Asian trade negotiations has meant that the largest bilateral flows of trade in the region are not yet covered by an FTA umbrella.

For the most part, the minilaterals that have emerged in the region in the last decade revolve around a series of ASEAN+1 agreements with China, Japan, Korea, India, and Australia/New Zealand. Broader agreements that would unite the entire region (such as the ASEAN+3 or ASEAN+6 initiatives) have yet to be implemented, as will be discussed in more detail later.

Cross-regionalism

Another striking trait of East Asian FTAs is their broad geographical reach. Although cross-regional trade agreements now crisscross the world, East Asia is notable for the early development of preferential trading links with extra-regional partners. In Europe and North America, the consolidation of the regional integration project (EC/EU, NAFTA) took precedence before cross-regional FTAs were pursued with vigor, but some of the early FTAs

Table 2 FTA strategies by country (as of February 2010)

	Under negotiation		Concluded				
	Framework agreement signed	Under negotiation	Signed	In effect	Total	Share of exports (%)	Top 5 FTA partners
Japan	0	5	2	9	11	25.6	ASEAN (11.8%), Thailand (3.5%), Singapore (3.0%), Malaysia (2.0%), Mexico (1.4%)
China	2	4	1	9	10	34.6	Hong Kong (16.0%), ASEAN (7.4%), Singapore (2.4%), Australia (1.4%), Thailand (1.0%)
Singapore	1	9	3	15	18	68.5	ASEAN (30.8%), US (10.1%), China (9.7%), Japan (5.4%), Australia (3.7%)
Korea	0	9	1	5	6	50.3	US (13.3%), ASEAN (9.8%), Singapore (2.9%), India (1.7%), Chile (0.5%)
Thailand	5	3	0	9	9	47.1	ASEAN (20.8%), Japan (12.6%), China (9.1%), Australia (3.4%), Korea (2.1%)
Philippines	1	1	0	5	5	34.9	ASEAN (17.3%), Japan (16.5%), China (9.8%), Australia (1.0%), New Zealand (0.1%)
Indonesia	2	1	1	5	6	42.9	Japan (21.6%), ASEAN (18.3%), China (8.3%), Australia (2.8%), New Zealand (0.3%)
Malaysia	2	6	1	6	7	43.0	ASEAN (26.1%), Japan (8.9%), China (7.3%), Korea (3.6%), India (3.2%)
India	5	7	1	8	9	21.0	Singapore (4.9%), Korea (1.9%), Sri Lanka (1.8%), S. Africa (1.7%), Bangladesh (1.4%)
Vietnam	1	2	1	4	5	39.3	ASEAN (16.6%), Japan (13.2%), Australia (9.4%), China (8.1%), Korea (2.1%)
Australia	1	5	0	7	7	30.1	China (12.3%), ASEAN (11.6%), US (6.2%), New Zealand (5.5%), Singapore (2.8%)

Source: IMF, Direction of Trade Statistics; ARIC, Free Trade Agreement for Asia and Integration Indicators Database.

Table 3 Competing views of integration

	US-Sing	J-Sing	J-ASEAN	C-ASEAN
Services	Yes	Yes	No	Limited, 2007
Investment	Yes	Yes	No	No
Govt. procurement	Yes	Yes	No	No
Competition policy	Yes	Yes	No	No
Intellectual property	Yes	Yes	No	No
Labor standards	Yes	No	No	No
Environment	Yes	No	No	No

Source: Compiled by the author from the text of the agreements and from the ADB database available at http://www.aric.adb.org/comparisonftacontent.php.

negotiated by East Asian nations were not with their neighbors but with distant partners (Singapore–US, Korea–Chile, Mexico–Japan, etc.). Table 1 emphatically makes this point, as close to 80% of all East Asian FTA initiatives are cross-regional.

This outward orientation in East Asian regionalism reflects a fundamental economic reality: the continued reliance on extra-regional markets to sustain export-oriented regional growth. As can be seen in Table 3, Korea and Singapore have moved more aggressively to negotiate FTAs with main markets of destination (the US, EU, and EFTA), ASEAN launched negotiations with the EU, but for Japan the goal of negotiating with the United States and the European Union has been difficult since Americans consider it unlikely that Japan will offer substantial agricultural liberalization, and Europeans worry about a major inflow of Japanese cars (Solís 2010). Besides market realities, East Asia's cross-regional FTA strategy also underscores significant regional obstacles to deeper integration as territorial and historical frictions and resource competition cloud inter-state negotiations (Solís and Katada 2007).

Hubs-and spokes

The familiar pattern of hubs-and-spokes that ensues with FTA proliferation is also discernible in East Asia, although there is some disagreement as to which countries qualify as 'hubs'. For instance, Kawai and Wignaraja (2009) count the number of FTAs that a country has signed to identify them as hubs. Following this criterion, the following countries pass the test: Singapore (18), Japan (11), China (10), India (9), and Korea (6).[6] However, for Baldwin (2008), hub status hinges on market size. In other words, the ability of a country to attract numerous FTA partners (and negotiate advantageous trade deals) depends on how much prospective FTA partners expect to increase their exports to that market with a preferential trade deal. The export magnification effect in turn is contingent on the share of bilateral exports and on the potential to increase market share (e.g., if a country already holds a 90% market share in the other nation's market, it is unlikely that an FTA will make much of a difference in improving its overall position there). For Baldwin, then, there are only two East Asian hubs, China and Japan, and East Asian regional integration is likely to adopt a bicycle shape, propelled by these two wheels.

In a series of moves and countermoves, Japan and China have competed vigorously in East Asia, enlisting trade partners in rival and overlapping FTA networks (Yang 2009; Solís 2009). However, the competitive courting of ASEAN has had surprising results from the conventional viewpoint in international trade negotiations that market size determines bargaining power. ASEAN – a collection of ten small economies that do not tightly coordinate their trade strategies (witness Singapore's and Thailand's forays into bilateralism for instance) – has emerged as the focal point of integration, dictating the terms of participation in the East Asian Summit and imprinting its FTAs with larger countries with a minimalist position vis-à-vis WTO-plus commitments. Political factors (in this case competition among would-be regional hegemons) seem to be important in opening space for smaller players to emerge as hubs.

Regional integration as a growth locomotive: An assessment of the challenges

The previous section revealed a distinct pattern in the evolution of East Asian regionalism where playing catch-up with the rest of the world in a situation of increasing uncertainty about the future of multilateral rounds of trade negotiations has spurred the regional FTA frenzy. After a decade of intense negotiations, numerous FTAs are already in place but these tend to be bilateral agreements that cover modest amounts of trade, many of them establish preferential links with extra-regional partners, and the competition is still on as to which countries will solidify their position as regional leaders.

Taking into account this panorama, this section discusses some of the challenges of shaping the existing maze of FTAs into a regional trade bloc capable of spurring dynamic growth as East Asia rethinks its developmental strategy.

Institutional design

A region-wide FTA that can truly energize trade and investment flows and reduce vulnerability to extra-regional shocks must overcome at least three major challenges: it must ensure the compatibility between network trade and FTA rules, it must increase intra-regional exports of final goods, and must encourage the involvement of the private sector by improving the quality of the agreements. Devising an FTA that can overcome all these hurdles is indeed a tall order.

Athukorala and Kohpaiboon (2009: 38–9) raise significant issues about the suitability of FTAs for regions characterized by fragmented production networks and high shares of component trade. On the one hand, the effect of tariff cuts is likely to be high in such cases as components cross borders frequently. In that sense a multiplier effect of tariff reduction can be expected to promote trade in particular in sectors such as automobiles and electronics where many East Asian countries still maintain relatively high tariffs (the Information and Technology Agreement for example does not include electric appliances in its tariff reduction schedule). On the other hand, the rules of origin (ROO) that are part-and-parcel of FTAs in order to avoid trade deflection could have significant deleterious effects for network trade. For starters, the costs of complying with customs procedures for a large number of part exports could significantly add to transaction costs. Moreover, many of the traded parts are low-value and therefore will have great difficulty in complying with regional value-added requirements, nor in many instances will they be able to comply with the criteria on 'change in tariff line' since they belong to the same HS code.

The prospects of China becoming in the medium to long term a magnet for imports of finished goods that can energize the regional economy are also uncertain. As Athukorala and Kohpaiboon (2009) point out, the countries in East Asia that experienced the sharpest export contraction during the global economic crisis (Japan, Korea, and Taiwan) are also the countries that trade most intensively with China. Growing commercial interdependence with China, therefore, has not insulated East Asian economies from sudden demand shocks in the industrialized world. For its part, China has adopted measures that seek to tap domestic demand as the main engine of growth: allocating funds in the stimulus package for social welfare, subsidizing retail sales of consumer durables such as electric appliances and automobiles, and the recent tolerance for modest currency appreciation that could enhance the purchasing power of consumers. Yet these steps are still modest given that the brunt of the stimulus package targeted infrastructure, that Chinese authorities are not willing to tolerate a major currency realignment that could compromise export competitiveness, and that the gap that China must fill is particularly high given that private consumption represents 35% of GDP while the international average is 50–70% (de Haan 2010; Eder et al. 2010; The Economist 2009).

Finally, the rate of business utilization of FTA preferences has received growing attention. Based on a survey of 609 firms operating in five East Asian countries (Japan, Korea, Singapore, Philippines, and Thailand), Kawai and Wignaraja (2009: 11–12) report that on average 22% of firms use the duty benefits. This figure is much higher than the rate of utilization of AFTA reported above, but still lower than FTA utilization rates in NAFTA or European FTAs (which can be as high as 60%). A lively debate has ensued on the reasons behind this gap. Kawai and Wignaraja (2009) note that in their survey the main obstacles cited by enterprises were insufficient knowledge about FTAs, low margins of tariff preference, and the administrative costs of complying with ROOs. They are therefore optimistic that as enterprises become more familiar with FTAs the utilization rates will increase. Others, however, believe that the reasons for low utilization run deeper and have to do primarily with the low quality of these agreements which then fail to elicit business involvement. Numerous exclusions of sensitive sectors,[7] lengthy calendars for liberalization, and reluctance to endorse WTO-plus commitments in investment, services, government procurement, and intellectual property are rampant flaws in many East Asian FTAs (Sally 2009). Ultimately, the priority attached by government officials to political considerations (avoid marginalization from ongoing regional diplomacy and/or appease powerful vested interests at home) as opposed to responding to the economic needs of business sectors, explains the low quality of these trade agreements (Ravenhill 2010; Solís 2010).

Multilateralizing challenges

With the rapid spread of bilateral FTAs the well-known problems of the noodle bowl effect and hub-and-spoke trap have also emerged in East Asia. Whether multilateralizing strategies can work will, therefore, loom large in the ability of the trade integration project to bring on board trade liberalization laggards (so they do not remain relegated to spoke status) and to simplify what could be an unwieldy maze of administrative red tape.

As Baldwin (2008) has explained, with bilateral preferential agreements the trade diversion effects will be greater, and the hub-and-spoke dynamic can marginalize the smaller economies while granting more leverage to the larger hub economies. These disadvantages derive from the fact that industrial investment will concentrate in the bigger economies within a free trade area, and that hubs will use to their advantage their larger market size to mold the FTA to suit their interests. The most effective strategy to avoid the spoke trap is to negotiate a customs union which eliminates the need for ROOs and ameliorates the disincentives for investing in the bloc's periphery.[8] Other possible strategies are for spokes to coordinate the negotiation of FTAs with the hub economy in order to achieve more bargaining leverage and obtain more homogenous agreements. Finally, a mid-sized developing economy can aim to become a hub by aggressively negotiating a string of FTAs with the largest markets in the world (e.g., Mexico's trade agreements with the United States, the EU, and Japan).

Another deleterious effect of FTA bilaterals is the proliferation of crisscrossing agreements with different liberalization calendars and diverging rules of origin (the so-called noodle bowl effect). There is no consensus on how restrictive are the rules of origin in East Asian FTAs. On the one hand, Manchin and Pelkmans-Balaoing (2007) posit that ROOs in East Asian

FTAs have significant trade-chilling effects since only very large preferential tariff margins (of roughly 25%) will compensate for the administrative cost of complying with origin certificates. On the other hand, Kawai and Wignaraja (2009: 13–14) note that in the survey mentioned before only a fraction of the firms (27%) complained that multiple ROOs increase their operating costs, and that a number of creative solutions (such as rules on cumulation, co-equality of ROOs, self-certification, etc.) can further ameliorate this problem. Baldwin (2006) is also optimistic on the chances of multilateralizing bilateral FTAs given Europe's experience in the late 1990s in developing a diagonal cumulation system.[9] Baldwin is confident that with the spread of fragmented manufacturing across borders, multinational corporations will lobby for the rationalization of cumbersome ROOs that will in effect multilateralize these agreements through the adoption of common ROO regimes.

The key question is whether these remedies can work for East Asia. The record so far is not promising. With respect to the anti-spoke strategies mentioned above, customs unions have been a rather rare phenomenon compared to the far more popular choice of shallower integration through FTAs. In East Asia there is no customs union in operation. Nor have the East Asian spokes coordinated their FTA negotiations vis-à-vis hub economies, and even in the ASEAN+1 FTAs the market access concessions are negotiated on a bilateral basis. On the other hand, Korea has been the East Asian country to pursue most actively the goal of becoming an FTA hub, but so far its strategy has been thwarted by the ratification limbo of its FTA with the United States and the deadlocked negotiations with Japan. It remains to be seen whether corporate demands to streamline rules of origin will make a difference. So far, discussion of cumulation schemes has not resulted in concrete initiatives to be implemented. Japan's own 'solution' (to negotiate an ASEAN-wide FTA to rationalize the ROOs of its bilateral agreements in Southeast Asia) is also a sobering reminder of the uphill road ahead as these negotiations dragged on for several years, and do not cover all of Japan's FTA network. Moreover, true multilateralization would require much more than tackling ROOs, as the trade and investment rules and principles that inform these FTAs vary significantly, as discussed next.

Architectural issues

The final set of challenges that the trade integration project faces revolve around broader 'foundational' questions regarding its breadth and depth. The main challenge arises from the fact that there are competing visions of what this integration process should be about in these two crucial dimensions:

a) Membership. The geographical boundaries of the trade bloc remain undefined, and at least three distinct possibilities are vying for support. China, for instance, has championed a purely East Asian bloc confined to the members of ASEAN+3, whereas Japan (probably attempting to dilute China's influence) vouched instead for an ASEAN+6 framework that also includes Australia, New Zealand, and India. On the other hand, while the prospects of negotiating an APEC FTA appear to be dim at this point, another Asia-Pacific initiative, the Trans-Pacific Partnership (TPP), has recently received more attention as a viable alternative for the United States to interject itself in the regional integration process. The political goal of influencing the direction of Asia-Pacific regionalism seems to be the overriding concern for the US decision to join the TPP given that it already has FTAs with many of its members (Elms 2009). Rather, the advantage of the TPP from the point of view of the United States is that it is compatible with its FTA template and has an open accession clause so that 'like minded' countries can join in.

Japan's announcement in autumn 2010 that it would consider joining the TPP negotiations could well provide further impetus to an Asia-Pacific integration track. Whether the Japanese government can overcome the steep domestic opposition to the large-scale liberalization entailed by TPP, especially in the aftermath of the earthquake, tsunami, and nuclear accident of March 2011, remains to be seen, but such development would significantly affect the existing battle among 'models' of integration. This competition has not only been about members, but also about what should be the desirable content of such trade negotiations.

b) Issue scope. As Table 3 shows, there are sharp differences on the issue scope of free trade agreements negotiated in the region. On the one hand, the United States has insisted on incorporating far-reaching WTO-plus commitments, and due to domestic pressures has tightened its demands on labor and environmental standards (they appeared as side agreements in NAFTA, but now must be included in the main body of the agreement and FTA partners must also comply with a number of international conventions as well) (Barfield and Levy 2009). Japan, on the other hand, has not been interested in linking labor and the environment to trade talks, but has aimed to disseminate a high-standard FTA model with multiple WTO-plus commitments to cover services, investment, intellectual property, and government procurement. Vis-à-vis China, Japan's FTAs are much more comprehensive in terms of issue scope as well as more legalistic (defining precise and binding obligations subject to dispute settlement). However, the contrast between Japan's FTAs with Singapore and ASEAN is revealing. Quite simply, in the ASEAN-wide FTA Japan was unable to exact WTO-plus commitments on services, investment, and government procurement. This outcome underscores the fact that a significant number of countries in the region (China and ASEAN) have little appetite for the deeper integration agenda.

East Asia, then, lacks a coherent vision of the end goal of trade integration, and the leadership contest is still raging as to which country will emerge as the focal point in the integration process, capable of fostering convergence on the terms of formalized economic cooperation.

Final remarks

This article has assessed the likely impact of the global economic crisis on the on-going process of formal trade integration in East Asia. This question is of interest for two reasons: 1) because theoretically there is no consensus as to whether economic contraction will hinder the chances of trade liberalization across all available trade forums; or whether the relative attractiveness of some forums (preferential trade agreements) will increase given that governments are better able to tailor the negotiation agenda to placate domestic interests and might be tempted to strive for regional encapsulation from external shocks; and 2) because Asian regionalism is very much the child of economic crisis, and the question arises whether this recent wave of economic turmoil will further fuel the integrationist flame in the region, and bring Asian trade integration to a new level.

The article found that the FTA frenzy shows no signs of abating in East Asia. The skepticism among regional elites about the chances of reactivating multilateral trade talks to foster recovery, the increasing emphasis in Asian policy circles on rebalancing Asian growth by promoting regional integration (in addition to nursing domestic demand), and burgeoning confidence in the region's potential as it has led the world in the path towards post-crisis recovery, have indeed opened political space to advance the cause of regional integration. And yet, even if state elites could seize this opportunity (as they did in the aftermath of the AFC to overcome the taboo on preferential trade negotiations) to launch the negotiation of a regional FTA, the chances of such a bloc becoming a true regional locomotive of growth are not bright.

Three sets of challenges complicate the chances of using a regional FTA to restructure East Asia's trade and investment flows in order to reduce over-dependence on extra-regional markets: a) institutional design issues point to the need to ensure the compatibility of FTAs with network trade, to increase business utilization of FTA preferences, and to find large consumption markets (e.g. China and/or Japan) to increase the intra-regional exports of finished goods; b) multilateralizing strategies to avoid the spoke-and-hub trap and the rising transaction costs of the noodle bowl such as the negotiation of customs unions and agreements on diagonal cumulation are yet to be attempted; and c) architectural issues on the most fundamental dimensions regarding breadth and depth of integration are still very much contested by the would-be leaders of the integration process. The track record of East Asian governments negotiating FTAs for diplomatic advantage abroad and political survival at home – without maximizing economic gains – does not bode well for the magnitude of this challenge.

The global recession has shed new light on one of the oldest debates on regional integration, if with added urgency: Should Asian countries aim to insulate themselves from adverse global trends (strive to decouple in a more deliberate fashion)? Or, on the contrary, given that East Asian regional production networks still depend on the American market, should preferential access to the United States be a top priority? The second option also faces the significant hurdle of bridging the disconnect between the US FTA template and regional preferences on trade integration. Muddling through – unappealing as it is – might be the default option as the region is confronted with this momentous crossroad.

Notes

1 Another major debate in the field focuses on the impact of the institutional setup of trade policymaking on the prospects for liberalization. A common view is that the Executive branch is less likely to be captured by narrow protectionist groups since the President faces a national electorate and is concerned with aggregate economic performance; while legislators must respond to local constituencies and through the dynamics of logrolling can sign on to very protectionist trade bills. The debate in this area has centered on the motivation for legislative delegation of trade policymaking to the Executive and the ability of the principal to control its agent (Destler 1992; O'Halloran 1994; De Bievre and Dur 2005).

2 In contrast, developing countries sign on to FTAs with industrialized nations (despite their weaker bargaining position) in order to secure access to large export markets and to outcompete other developing nations in capturing FDI inflows. These economic benefits are all the more important during periods of slow growth.

3 A study by the International Food Policy Research Institute estimates that if all countries reverted to their higher bound tariffs (a WTO-legal move) the contraction in world trade would be 7.7%, resulting in a loss of world income in the order of $353 billion (cited in Dadush 2009: 6).

4 Although trade is considered the main contagion channel, East Asian economies were also affected by the drying up of extra-regional financial flows as banks in the West attempted to repair their balance sheets, and institutional investors curtailed their operations, resulting in a net equity outflow (IMF 2009b). Japan in particular was the industrialized nation most affected by the crisis (recording negative growth rates in 2008) due to structural changes over the past decade (with increasing exposure to international trade, and an export profile based almost entirely on income-elastic products) (Kawai and Takagi 2009).

5 As with previous episodes of financial crisis, there is plenty of blame circulating on both sides of the Pacific. Some Western observers have emphasized Asia's 'savings glut' and the excessive accumulation of foreign exchange reserves (principally by China) as enabling factors encouraging the consumption binge and speculative real estate deals in the United States; whereas Asian observers have focused mainly on the financial regulatory failures of the United States. For further details on this debate see Plummer (2009) and Wolf (2008).

6 Interestingly, the share of exports covered by FTAs is not very high given the numerous such agreements that these countries have signed. The highest shares of exports under FTAs are for Singapore (68.5%), Korea (50.3%), and Thailand (47.1%). What we are witnessing in East Asia is, therefore, a multiplication of small bilaterals.

7 Measuring the degree of exclusions across all East Asian FTAs is a difficult task. Kawai and Wignaraja (2009: 15–16) have developed classification criteria on agricultural liberalization whereby 'comprehensive coverage' applies to agreements that include 85% of agricultural tariff lines or where no more than 150 lines are excluded. This classification can be too permissive, however, since for example the Korea–Chile FTA qualifies, even though the agreement excludes the most important agricultural staple for Korea – rice.

8 This dynamic was at work when NAFTA's stiff rules of origin in automobiles and mandated elimination of duty drawback programs in Canada and Mexico created a disincentive for Japanese investment in these nations (Solís 1995).

9 Baldwin (2006: 31) provides a clear definition of diagonal cumulation: 'Once a product enters the diagonal cumulation zone, its origin is determined by the common ROOs and it can never lose its origin status by crossing a border internal to the zone. This means that ROOs cease to influence the choice of suppliers among nations that are members of the zone.'

References

Ahearn, R. J. (2009) 'The global economic downturn and protectionism', CRS Report for Congress, accessed at http://assets.opencrs.com/rpts/R40461_20090323.pdf, 7 January 2010.

Ahn, C. (2010) 'Weathering the storm: the impact of the global financial crisis on Asia', *Global Asia*, accessed at http://www.globalasia.org/print.php?c=e267, 3 August 2010.

Alt, J. and Gilligan, M. (1994) 'The political economy of trading states: factor specificity, collective action problems, and domestic political institutions', *Journal of Political Philosophy* 2(2): 165–92.

Asian Development Bank (ADB) (2009) 'The global economic crisis: challenges for developing Asia and the ADB's response', accessed at http://www.adb.org/Documents/Reports/Economic-Crisis/Global-Economic-Crisis-042709.pdf, 14 June 2009.

Asian Development Bank (ADB) (2010) 'Asia Economic Monitor' (July), accessed at http://aric.adb.org/pdf/aem/jul10/Jul_AEM_regional.pdf, 5 August 2010.

Athukorala, P. and Kohpaiboon, A. (2009) 'Intra-regional trade in East Asia: the decoupling fallacy, crisis, and policy challenges', ADBI Working Paper Series, no. 177 (December), 44 pp., accessed at http://www.adbi.org/files/2009.12.11.wp177.intra.regional.trade.east.asia.pdf, 4 January 2010.

Baldwin, R. E. (2006) 'Multilateralizing regionalism: spaghetti bowls as building blocs on the path to global free trade', *The World Economy* 29: 1451–518.

Baldwin, R. E. (2007) 'Managing the noodle bowl: the fragility of East Asian regionalism', ADB Working Paper Series on Regional Economic Integration, no. 7 (February), accessed at http://aric.adb.org/pdf/workingpaper/WP07_Baldwin.pdf, 22January 2010.

Baldwin, R. E. (2008) 'The spoke trap: hub-and-spoke bilateralism in East Asia', in B. Eichengreen, Y. C. Park and C. Wyplosz (eds)*China, Asia, and the New World Economy*, Oxford: Oxford University Press, pp. 51–85.

Baldwin, R. E. and Evenett S. (2009) 'The collapse of global trade, murky protectionism, and the crisis: recommendations for the G20', A VoxEU publication, accessed at http://www.unisg.ch/hsgweb.nsf/SysWebRessources/Evenett,+Simon:+The+collapse+of+global+trade,+murky+protectionism,+and+the+crisis:+Recommendations+for+the+G20/$FILE/Murky_Protectionism.pdf, 20 October 2009.

Barfield, C. and Levy P. I. (2009) 'Tales of the South Pacific: President Obama and the transpacific partnership', *American Enterprise Institute for Public Policy Research* 2(December): 9 pp.

Bhagwati, J. (2008) *Termites in the Trading System: How Preferential Trade Agreements Undermine Free Trade*, New York: Oxford University Press.

Bowles, P. (2002) 'Asia's post-crisis regionalism: bringing the state back in, keeping the (United) States out', *Review of International Political Economy* 9(2): 244–70.

Brawley, M. R. (2006) 'Agricultural interests, trade adjustment, and repeal of the Corn Laws', *British Journal of Politics and International Relations* 8(4): 467–88.

Busch, M. (2007) 'Overlapping institutions, forum shopping, and dispute settlement in international trade', *International Organization* 61: 735–61.

Bussiere, M., Pérez-Barreiro, M., Straub, R. and Taglioni, D. (2009) 'Protectionist responses to the crisis: global trends and implications', accessed at http://enviroscope.iges.or.jp/modules/envirolib/staff_view.php?sid=258, 14 January 2009.

Chase, K. (2003) 'Economic interests and regional trading arrangements: the case of NAFTA', *International Organization* 57(1): 137–74.

China View (2009) 'Singapore FM: persisting regional integration crucial amid economic downturn', 26 February.

Condliffe, J. B. (1940) *The Reconstruction of World Trade*, New York: W. W. Norton.

Dadush, U. (2009) 'Resurgent protectionism: risks and possible remedies', Policy Outlook. Carnegie Endowment for International Peace, accessed at http://www.carnegieendowment.org/files/Resurgent_Protectionism.pdf, 11 January 2010.

Davis, C. L. (2009) 'Overlapping institutions in trade policy', *Perspectives on Politics* 7(1): 25–31.

De Bievre, D. and Dur, A. (2005) 'Constituency interests and delegation in European and American trade policy', *Comparative Political Studies* 38(10): 1271–96.

De Haan, A. (2010) 'A defining moment? China's social policy response to the financial crisis', *Journal of International Development* 22: 758–71.

Destler, I. M. (1992) *American Trade Politics*, Washington, DC: Institute for International Economics.

Eder, G., Grimm, M. and Steck, G. (2010) 'Asia – outlook after the crisis', Allianz Working Paper no. 138 (May), accessed at https://www.allianz.com/static-resources/en/economic_research/images_englisch/pdf_downloads/working_papers/asien-e0510.pdf, 9 August 2010.

Elms, D. (2009) 'From the P4 to the TPP: explaining expansion of interests in the Asia-Pacific', paper for Asia Pacific Trade Economists' Conference. Bangkok, 2–3 November, accessed at http://www.unescap.org/tid/artnet/mtg/Deborah%20Elms.pdf, 12 January 2010.

Erixon, F. and Sally, R. (2009) 'Fighting the urge for protectionism', *Far Eastern Economic Review* (January–February): 28–31.

Stratfor (2010) 'Forget about the consumer revolution, China has a long way to go', 26 April, accessed at http://www.businessinsider.com/stratfor-china-consumer-2010-4, 4 August 2010.

Gamberoni, E. and Newfarmer, R. (2009) 'Trade protection: incipient but worrisome trends', *World Bank Trade Notes*, no. 37, March, accessed at http://siteresources.worldbank.org/NEWS/Resources/Trade_Note_37.pdf, 17 January 2010.

Gill, B., Green, M., Tsuji, K. and Watts, W. (2009) 'Strategic views on Asian regionalism', CSIS Report (February), accessed at http://csis.org/files/media/csis/pubs/090217_gill_stratviews_web.pdf, 7 January 2010.

Grossman, G. M. and Helpman, E. (1995) 'The politics of free-trade agreements', *The American Economic Review* 85(4): 667–90.

Hiscox, M. (2003) 'Class versus industry cleavages: inter-industry factor mobility and the politics of trade', *International Organization* 55(1): 1–46.

International Monetary Fund (IMF) (2009a) 'World economic outlook', accessed at http://www.imf.org/external/pubs/ft/weo/2009/02/pdf/text.pdf, 26 January 2010.

International Monetary Fund (IMF) (2009b) 'Asia and Pacific. Global crisis: the Asian context', Regional economic outlook, accessed at http://www.imf.org/external/pubs/ft/reo/2009/APD/eng/areo0509.pdf, 20 October 2009.

Katada, S. and Solís, M. (2010) 'Domestic sources of Japanese foreign policy activism: loss avoidance and demand coherence', *International Relations of the Asia-Pacific* 10: 129–57.

Kawai, M. (2009) 'The impact of the global financial crisis on Asia and Asia's responses', paper presented at the AEEF Conference, Kiel (July), accessed at http://www.bruegel.org/fileadmin/files/admin/research_initiatives/asia_europe_economic_forum/AEEF_July_2009/paperKawai_Global_Financial_Crisis_and_Asia__Responses_AEEF_Kiel_7July09_07-06-2009__4_pdf, 7 January 2010.

Kawai, M. and Takagi, S. (2009) 'Why was Japan hit so hard by the global financial crisis', ADBI Working Paper Series, no. 153, October, accessed at http://www.adbi.org/working-paper/2009/10/05/3343.japan.gfc/, 17 January 2010.

Kawai, M. and Wignaraja, G. (2009) 'Asian FTAs: trends and challenges', ADBI Working Paper Series, no. 144 (August), accessed at http://www.adbi.org/working-paper/2009/08/04/3256.asian.fta.trends.challenges/, 20 January 2010.

Kim, S., Lee, J. W. and Park, C.Y. (2009) 'Emerging Asia: decoupling or recoupling?', ADB Working Paper Series on Regional Economic Integration, no. 31 (June), accessed at http://aric.adb.org/pdf/workingpaper/WP31_Decoupling_or-Recoupling.pdf, 8 December 2009.

Lord, M. (2009) 'Is Asian integration sheltering the region from the crisis?', Background discussion paper for ECFIN Conferences (October), accessed at http://beyondtheglobalcrisis.eu/Doc/Microsoft%20Word%20-%20Revised%20final%20version%20paper%20Lord%2002-Oct-2009.PDF, 6 December 2009.

MacIntyre, A., Pempel, T. J. and Ravenhill, J. (eds) (2008) *Crisis as Catalyst: Asia's Dynamic Political Economy*, Ithaca, NY: Cornell University Press.

Manchin, M. and Pelkmans-Balaoing, A. O. (2007) 'Rules of origin and the web of East Asian free trade agreements', World Bank Policy Research Working Paper, no. 4273 (July), accessed at http://www-wds.worldbank.org/external/default/WDSContentServer/IW3P/IB/2007/07/06/000016406_20070706154708/Rendered/PDF/wps4273.pdf, 9 February 2010.

Mansfield, E. D. and Milner, H. V. (1999) 'The new wave of regionalism', *International Organization* 53(3): 589–627.

Milner, H. V. (1999) 'The political economy of international trade', *Annual Review of Political Science* 2: 91–114.

Milner, H. V. (1997) 'Industries, governments, and the creation of regional trading blocs', in E. D. Mansfield and H. V. Milner (eds) *The Political Economy of Regionalism*, New York: Columbia University Press, pp. 77–106.

Munakata, N. (2006) *Transforming East Asia. The Evolution of Regional Economic Integration*, Washington, DC: Brookings Institution Press.

O'Halloran, S. (1994) *Politics, Process and American Trade Policy*, Ann Arbor: University of Michigan Press.

Pekkanen, S., Solís, M. and Katada, S. (2007) 'Trading gains for control: international trade forums and Japanese economic diplomacy', *International Studies Quarterly* 51(4): 945–70.

Pempel, T. J. and Urata, S. (2006) 'Japan: a new move toward bilateral trade agreements', in V. Aggarwal and S. Urata (eds) *Bilateral Trade Agreements in the Asia-Pacific*, New York and London: Routledge, pp. 75–94.

Plummer, M. G. (2009) 'The global economic crisis and its implications for Asian economic cooperation', East–West Center Policy Studies no. 55, accessed at http://www.eastwestcenter.org/fileadmin/stored/pdfs/ps055.pdf, 16 January 2010.

Pula, G. and Peltonen, T. A. (2009) 'Has emerging Asia decoupled? An analysis of production and trade linkages using the Asian International Input–Output Table', European Central Bank Working Paper Series, no. 993 (January), accessed at http://www.ecb.eu/pub/pdf/scpwps/ecbup993.pdf, 4 December 2009.

Ravenhill, J. (2010) 'The "new East Asian regionalism": a political domino', *Review of International Political Economy* 17(2): 178–208.

Rogowski, R. (1989) *Commerce and Coalitions: How Trade Affects Domestic Political Alignments*, Princeton, NJ: Princeton University Press.

Sally, R. (2009) 'Regional economic integration in Asia: the track record and prospects', paper presented at PAFTAD 33 Conference, Taipei (October), accessed at http://www.ecipe.org/people/razeen-sally/other-publications/asiaregintegrationaug09.pdf, 29 January 2010.

Solís, M. (1995) 'La inversión japonesa directa en México y Canada: compartimos los efectos negativos de la integración económica?' [Japanese direct investment in Mexico and Canada: do we share the negative effects of economic integration?], in G. Vega (ed.) *Mexico, Estados Unidos, Canada, 1993–1994*, México: El Colegio de México.

Solís, M. (2004) *Banking on Multinationals: Public Credit and the Export of Japanese Sunset Industries*, Stanford, CA: Stanford University Press.

Solís, M. (2009) 'Japan's competitive FTA strategy: commercial opportunity versus political rivalry', in M. Solís, B. Stallings and S. N. Katada (eds) *Competitive Regionalism: FTA Diffusion in the Pacific Rim*, Basingstoke: Palgrave Macmillan, pp. 198–215.

Solís, M. (2010) 'Can FTAs deliver market liberalization in Japan? A study on domestic political determinants' *Review of International Political Economy* 17(2): 209–37.

Solís, M. and Katada, S. N. (2007) 'Understanding East Asian cross-regionalism: an analytical framework', *Pacific Affairs* 80(2): 229–57.

Solís, M. and Katada, S. N. (2009) 'Explaining FTA proliferation: a policy diffusion framework', in M. Solís, B. Stallings and S. N. Katada (eds) *Competitive Regionalism: FTA Diffusion in the Pacific Rim*, Basingstoke: Palgrave Macmillan, pp. 1–24.

Tackacs, W. (1981) 'Pressures for protectionism: an empirical analysis', *Economic Inquiry* 19: 687–93.

The Economist. (2009) 'Shopaholics wanted: Can Asians replace Americans as a driver of global growth?', June 25. Available online at http://www.economist.com/node/13900125.

Van Grasstek, C. (2009) 'Building without BRICs: lessons from the "buy American" debate', *Bridges* 13(1), accessed at http://ictsd.org/downloads/bridges/bridges13-1.pdf, 19 January 2010.

Yang, J. (2009) 'China's Competitive FTA Strategy: Realism on a Liberal Slide', in M. Solís, B. Stallings and S. N. Katada (eds) *Competitive Regionalism: FTA*

Diffusion in the Pacific Rim, Houndmills, Basingstoke: Palgrave Macmillan, pp. 216–35.

Wolf, M. (2008) *Fixing Global Finance*, Baltimore, MD: Johns Hopkins University Press.

World Trade Organization (WTO) (2009) 'Overview of developments in the international trading system. Annual report by the Director General', accessed at http://www.wto.org/english/news_e/news09_e/wt_tpr_ov_12_b_e.doc, 11 January 2010.

Rethinking the Beijing Consensus: how China responds to crises

Yang Jiang

Abstract This paper discusses the role of the Beijing Consensus type of foreign and economic policymaking in China's development since the Asian financial crisis and in its response to the global crisis, and argues that it has been a double-edged sword, as reflected in several aspects. First, the lesson that China learned from the Asian financial crisis was not the importance of liberalisation but prudence or conservativeness, which despite serving as a shield this time sustains problems in the long term. Second, an obsession with foreign reserves accumulation and the pursuit of political influence have for a long time overshadowed the increasing dependence on the US market, putting China in a dilemma now in both development and diplomatic strategies. Third, centralised decision-making may be faster than democratic processes, but it may also go against the principle of 'scientific decision' as proposed by the Chinese leadership. A prominent feature of China's responses to the crisis is a bias towards state-owned enterprises and the public sector, which exacerbates the existing problems of monopoly, over-capacity, inequality, the regulators being 'captured' by industrial interests and protectionism. Given limited economic resources, domestic political contentions and the questionable credibility of the China Model, it would be difficult for China to practice 'responsible great power' diplomacy or assume leadership in the region or globally.

Yang Jiang is Assistant Professor at Asia Research Centre, Copenhagen Business School. Originally from China, she got her PhD from the Australian National University, and mainly works on the domestic policymaking of China's foreign economic policy. She has published in *Review of International Political Economy*, *The Pacific Review*, *The Journal of Contemporary China*, *Australian Journal of International Affairs*, and *Copenhagen Journal of Asian Studies*.

1. Introduction

Beijing may laugh at the Washington Consensus floundering in the global financial crisis, but is it possible that China has fallen into the trap of the Beijing Consensus?

Following the Asian financial crisis, the global financial crisis provided China with another golden opportunity to undermine the Washington Consensus, on the one hand by justifying its political economic system for domestic development, and on the other hand by introducing its development model to other countries. China defends its political system for maintaining domestic stability, fitting the supposedly Confucius culture, and for being able to make and carry out decisions swiftly. Beijing also is also proud of its development path for rapid economic growth, and upholds Deng Xiaoping's wisdom of 'crossing the river by feeling the stones'. In a survey of 300 Chinese officials in March 2009, 75% believed that the China Model had undermined 'three predictions' made by the West: communism or socialism would die, Western democracy would prevail, and neoliberalism would be a universal model (*Renmin Luntan* 2009). The Western media also praised China for its swiftness in introducing stimulus packages, which were regarded as helpful for boosting confidence in the global market and particularly beneficial to regional economies. Particularly in contrast to the protracted process of congressional approval in Washington, the ability of Beijing to take quick action is deemed superior for crisis response.

In its foreign relations, since it gained a lot of political capital by maintaining the value of the renminbi (RMB) during the 1997–98 Asian financial crisis, China has positioned itself as a 'responsible great power' (*fuzeren daguo*) in the region and in the world. China praises itself for 'great power style' (*daguo fengfan*), which is opposite to the predatory great powers. In particular, Chinese leaders emphasise China's generosity in allowing smaller countries the advantage in their cooperation and its determination to speak for developing countries at global institutions, an image that bears resemblance to the Western concept of benign hegemony. Beijing points out that the imposition of conditionalities by the International Monetary Fund (IMF) and World Bank on developing countries have destroyed more than ten national economies including Argentina and Indonesia, particularly thanks to neoliberal economic doctrines embedded in the Washington Consensus in combination with the ensuing modern financial industry and greed. The Chinese government and academia proudly claim that China never attaches conditionalities to its aid or loans to other developing countries and it does not intervene in domestic politics. Many developing countries, including those in Africa, have expressed their appreciation of China's non-intervention in their domestic affairs, and their intention to learn from China's development model, for instance by establishing Special Economic Zones and encouraging labour-intensive manufacturing, with the help of Chinese loans, investment and experience.

However, the role of the Beijing Consensus in China's domestic development needs more scrutiny before it can be introduced to other developing nations or indeed lauded within China. Moreover, the image of a benign hegemon is more difficult to sustain in economic crisis as great powers may become more nationalistic and vulnerable.

Therefore, this paper analyzes the ideational and institutional factors behind China's development since the Asian financial crisis and behind its response to the global financial crisis, and discusses the implications of domestic conditions for Chinese diplomacy. It asks the following questions: how has the 'Beijing Consensus' type of development strategy and policymaking affected China's response to the global financial crisis; and what implications do they have for Chinese 'responsible great power' diplomacy?

The rest of the paper is organized as follows. After reviewing the existing literature on the Beijing Consensus and China's responsible great power diplomacy, it analyzes the ideational impacts that the Asian financial crisis had on China. The lessons learned by China then serve as a background to the discussion of China's response to the global financial crisis in the next section, focusing on three major problems: the concentration of distributional power and the resultant 'unscientific' decisions, the bias towards state-owned enterprises, and continued reliance on labour-intensive manufacturing and export. Finally, the implications of the 'Beijing Consensus' type of policymaking and development strategy for China's regional and global diplomacy are discussed, assessing the distance of China from its aspired status of a responsible great power.

2. Literature review

Although the 'China Model' was mentioned as early as 1991, the term 'Beijing Consensus' was dubbed by former *Time* editor Joshua Cooper Ramo (2004) as a challenge to 'the Washington Consensus', and Beijing Consensus (*Beijing gongshi*) has been used interchangeably with the term the China Model (*zhongguo moshi*). Ramo's association of the Beijing Consensus with innovation, sustainability and equitable development is hardly adequate, but despite that or because of it, the Politburo of the China Communist Party (CCP), the core of China's decision-making power, quickly welcomed the spread of the terms 'Beijing Consensus' and 'China Model' in the international media, as they were believed to help enhance China's soft power (Liaowang 2004). However, after the media attention turned to its revisionist connotations, the Chinese government denied that China was trying to teach the China Model to other developing countries or to challenge the existing international order. It states that the China Model means there is no one model for a country; rather, each country needs to search for its own development or political model.

Chinese academia has been debating whether there is one China Model, with many denying this concept (http://theory.people.com.cn/GB/40557/

149513/ index.html; also see Kennedy 2010). China watchers compare the influence of the Washington Consensus and that of the Beijing Consensus, commenting on the soft power of the latter and its threat to the existing international order (Kurlantzick 2007; Kroeber 2008; Rachman 2008). Some have found fault with the Beijing Consensus, mostly in authoritarianism, human rights records, income inequality, a withering state and corruption (Gill and Huang 2006; Kennedy 2010; Yao 2010). Although there is no academic consensus over the definition of the Beijing Consensus or the China Model, this paper uses the official Chinese position for analysis of its policies and holds that the Chinese government has explicitly or implicitly given two important meanings to the Beijing Consensus or the China Model: gradualist development and authoritarian decision-making.

Crises put models to good test. Protectionism is one general concern, and whether great powers are willing and able to provide public goods is another. Despite much rhetoric regarding China's superior model and great power style during the global financial crisis, to date these has not been a study of the role of the China Model in its response to the crisis, and its implications for China's 'responsible great power' diplomacy. Neither has China's response to the global crisis been contextualized in China's development trajectory, in particular its lessons from the Asian financial crisis at the end of the 1990s. Therefore this paper seeks to fill these gaps, with the acknowledgement that the aftermath of the global financial crisis is still rippling, and China's policies may undergo significant changes due to serious external economic pressure, domestic instability or iron-fisted idealistic leaders.

Since the Asian financial crisis, Beijing has tried to establish an image of a 'responsible great power' and demonstrates 'great power style', ostensibly used in contrast to other great powers and the US in particular. Eric Teo (2004) suggests that China was trying to revive the tributary system in Asia, and the title 'the Middle Kingdom' has appeared frequently in the recent media. China has denied such observations, claiming never to pursue hegemony and emphasizing equality among sovereign states. However, Chinese leaders have heralded Confucianism, the core value in the ancient tributary system, for building a harmonious world. China prides itself on its generosity, compassion and sense of responsibility in its diplomacy in Asia and towards other developing countries. Chinese officials emphasize mutual benefit but also claim to follow the ancient tradition of 'giving more and receiving less' (*hou wang bo lai*) in its diplomacy towards smaller countries. Clearly China wishes to achieve the symbolic status of a great power, both in economic and military strength and in cultural and moral achievements. The model that China wishes others to admire and to emulate and the symbolic status that Beijing aspires to resemble the Western concept of benign hegemony (Kindleberger 1975; Kupchan 1998). It is questionable, however, whether China can carry out the responsibilities of a benign hegemon: providing public goods and creating international institutions.

As diplomacy serves China's domestic needs and diplomatic ambitions are constrained by domestic conditions, it is crucial to examine China's domestic political economy and crisis policymaking. There have been criticisms from both within and outside China on the risks with China's crisis rescue measures, predominantly from an economic point of view: excessive debt, inflation and real estate bubbles (e.g. Yao 2010; Kennedy 2010). Less attention has been paid to the political and institutional factors behind those measures, or the continuity of China's policies since the Asian financial crisis. The existing or potential economic woes may have institutional, ideational and political roots that are more persistent than the vicissitudes of economic environments.

While Keynesianism enjoys a renewed interest in developed countries during the global financial crisis, the Beijing Consensus or China Model is placed as an exemplary model for developing and Asian economies. Indeed, Chinese finance officials and scholars have cited Keynes in the wake of the global financial crisis, and the prominent role the Chinese state plays in the economy appears similar to Keynesianism (Zhou 2009; Fan 2010). However, China has achieved too little in domestic income redistribution and social security to qualify as a Keynesian state. In its economic representations, the Beijing Consensus resonates more with East Asian developmental state in terms of heavy state intervention, gradualist liberalization and state-backed industrial policies, focused on promotion of export and national enterprises (Baek 2005; Beeson 2009; Kerr 2007). Pioneered by Japan and followed to varying degrees by East Asian economies, the developmental state was once regarded as the core of the 'East Asian Miracle' (Amsden 2001; Terry 2002; World Bank 1993; Stubbs 2005). However, disillusionment with this miracle emerged during the Asian financial crisis, when the developmental state became closely associated with crony capitalism (Higgott 1998; Noble and Ravenhill 2000; Stubbs 2005). Certainly, putting the blame on neoliberal measures has continued in crisis-hit countries, but with Japan's protracted stagnation and the neoliberal reforms of other smaller East Asian economies, the developmental state has only met the opportunity of revival during the global financial crisis. Perhaps because the phrase 'developmental state' is accredited to its political rival in Tokyo, Beijing prefers to use the terms 'China Model' or 'Beijing Consensus'. It raises the question whether the typical problems with the developmental model exist in China. Many scholars have pointed out that Beijing's reliance on economic growth for its legitimacy may not be sustainable, given rising social inequality and public discontent (e.g. Breslin 2007; He 2007; Schubert 2008). Yang Yao (2010), in his provocative article 'The End of the Beijing Consensus', correctly states that in the past 30 years China has moved toward the market doctrines of neoclassical economics. However, he argues that the Chinese state survived as a Marxist regime because the state's 'predation is "identity-blind" in the sense that Beijing does not generally care about the social and political status of its chosen prey – unlike many governments elsewhere that act to protect and enrich specific social or political groups'. The 'indifference' that he and other scholars characterize the Chinese state with is debatable. Because of development strategy and partial reform, it is possible that even an authoritarian China is captured by certain vested interests, which inhibits further reform and induces policies that exacerbate inequality (Hellman 1998; Feng 2006). The crisis is a good time to investigate whether Beijing has indeed favoured the embedded interests.

The next section will analyze the lessons that China learned from the Asian financial crisis, which serves as a context and explanation for its response to the global financial crisis. The aim is to examine if and to what extent China's Beijing Consensus type of thinking and policymaking have contributed to recurring or even exacerbating problems.

3. What China learned from the Asian financial crisis

China was affected by the Asian financial crisis in terms of reduced exports and foreign investment, but the most important impact the crisis had on China was ideational. The lessons that China learned from other countries and its own experiences during the crisis have since guided Chinese development and diplomatic strategies and only recently received significant doubt. There are three major lessons: desirability of a responsible great power status, caution about financial liberalization and a strategy to promote exports for economic security and growth.

3.1. Desirability of a responsible great power status

China gained a lot of political capital by keeping the value of the yuan and delivering aid to countries hit by the Asian financial crisis (M. Wang 1998; Y. Wang 1998). China stressed that had it devalued the yuan, international speculators would have again attacked the foreign exchange and stock markets of other East Asian countries. Although China's lack of support for the Japanese proposal of an Asian Monetary Fund was a major reason for the proposal's failure, China realised the importance of participating in regional institution building. Chinese policymakers discovered that Japan's New Miyazawa Initiative in 1998, a US$30 billion financial assistance package for the region, was welcomed by Southeast Asian countries, and that Japan's influence in East Asia increased (Sun 2007). Having come under pressure from other Asian countries, China also foresaw that certain mechanism for regional cooperation would inevitably be established, even possibly without the participation of China (author's interview with a Chinese member at the Pacific Economic Cooperation Council (PECC), Beijing, April 2007). This realisation, together with the positive response China received from ASEAN for keeping the value of RMB, prompted China to adopt a more committed stance in regional cooperation. Despite Deng Xiaoping's advice for Chinese diplomacy to '*tao guang yang hui*' (hide the sharpness and accumulate strength), Chinese foreign policymakers judged that it was time for China to also '*yu shi ju jin*' (follow the trend of time) and '*you suo zuo wei*' (achieve something).

Since Zoellick (2005) prescribed the role of a 'responsible stakeholder' in the international system for China, the emphasis on China being a responsible member in the region and in the global society has become increasingly prominent in Chinese official language. Chinese leaders have, on various occasions, underlined China's friendship towards its neighbours and its sense of responsibility for the region. A Chinese phrase that the Chinese leaders often quote goes 'a long road shows the power of a horse, and a long time shows the heart of people' (*luyao zhi mali, rijiu jian renxin*), implying that China's friendship towards its neighbours and other developing countries have passed the test of time, while some Western countries failed. A central claim from the contrast is that China is not a predatory coercive power or hegemony. China argues that its contribution to the region during the crisis showed that China was becoming a great global economic power, but it was under-represented at international financial institutions such as the World Bank, the IMF and the Asian Development Bank (ADB). Beijing also started to highlight its 'great power style', which was to 'give more and take less' and shoulder collective responsibilities. China has since lauded itself for the great power style on various occasions, for example, when China kept the value of RMB during the Asian financial crisis, when it exempted Africa from US$10 billion of debts in 2000, and when Chinese leaders went on shopping sprees across continents during the global financial crisis.

3.2. Caution about financial liberalization

China did not experience a financial or economic crisis when the Asian financial crisis hit most countries in the region, characterized by massive outflow of international short-term capital, sharp devaluation of the national currencies and difficulty with balance of payments. Many Chinese policy elites realized the necessity of economic reform to strengthen domestic institutions and to enhance national competitiveness. In Steinfeld's view (2008), the Asian financial crisis helped the formation of an ideational environment in China that enabled members of the Chinese policy elite like Premier Zhu Rongji to push forward more radical and fundamental market reforms. As a result, China's agenda of 'reform as the salvation of socialism' became replaced by 'markets as the salvation of growth and legitimacy'.

At the same time, Chinese policymakers and scholars became more vigilant of the pitfalls in financial liberalization. Chinese scholars point out that the fundamental reason for the crisis was the inconsistency between domestic reforms and the premature liberalization of the financial market.

Therefore, it is widely held that developing countries should balance reform and liberalization, and that trade integration has more benefits for developing countries than financial integration. In particular, the liberalization of the financial sector should be coherent with the country's economic development and supervisory ability; it should be even more cautious in opening the capital market (Y. Wang 1998; Xiao 2006; Breslin 2003). They believe that China should conduct financial reform in a stable and active manner, and form a financial surveillance system. Moreover, they hold that the crisis did not happen to China despite problems with Chinese banks because China had capital controls, and that giving up capital controls should therefore be the last step of all marketization reforms, after domestic financial institutions have become strong enough to handle international risks and China has established the mechanism to monitor international capital flows, in particular the short-term ones, and it should be done only after floating the currency (Yu 2007). The consensus in China has been that it should only gradually float the yuan because it is believed that the overall health of the national economy is heavily dependent on trade and domestic savings. In particular, Chinese scholars suggest that China should not allow international free capital – or 'hot money' – to enter or leave China freely, for instance by having restrictions on foreign loans of domestic companies and local governments, and that Chinese banks should not allow loans that are not certain to be returned in the future (Fan 1999; Zhong 2008).

Importantly, Chinese scholars criticize the Washington Consensus – with neoliberal economics at the centre – regarding economic reform and liberalization as being not necessarily safe or helpful to East Asian economies, and they hold that China should use discretion when it listens to the advice of the IMF. The reason, they argue, is that privatization and liberalization cannot prevent financial crises but may aggravate or even cause them if not accompanied by comprehensive regulation and supervision. Ding Ningning at the Development Studies Centre of the State Council states that financial internationalization and electronic means of transactions have not increased the transparency of the international market but have exacerbated its instability (Y. Wang 1998).

3.3. Promote export for economic security and growth

Because of the devaluation of regional currencies and hence the reduced purchasing power of consumers in the neighbouring countries, China's growth rate of exports to East Asia declined significantly during the financial crisis. Instead of questioning the export-led model of growth (Breslin 1999), China chose the path to increase exports. One objective was to accumulate foreign reserves in order to prevent anything like the Asian financial crisis from happening to China in the future. Another objective, by accepting the transfer of exports of other Asian countries from the US, EU and Japan to China, China would increase its influence in Asia and promote the image of a responsible great power (author's interviews with scholars at CASS, Beijing University and Ministry of Commerce officials in March and April 2006 in Beijing).

The obsession with accumulating foreign reserves combined with the political will to provide 'market of last resort' for Asian countries thus led to increased reliance of the Chinese economy on export markets in developed countries like the US and EU (Ravenhill 2006). This model continues to bode poorly for China's industrialization, as most Chinese activities in the production chain are low value-added processing.

Further results from this growth model are apparent: pressure from other countries on Beijing to appreciate the RMB, trade disputes, inflation, and an increasing need for multiple markets. Inflation has caused domestic instability in recent years and the government has to use administrative measures to control prices, particularly those of food. In order to gain access to multiple markets, Beijing is actively pursuing bilateral trade agreements, most of which are with developing countries. Even though China tries to show that it has the great power morality of giving more and taking less in trade agreements, including voluntarily giving concessions to ASEAN and Pakistan on agricultural trade through the Early Harvest Programmes, such arrangements cannot completely convince smaller countries of China's benign intentions. For instance, while the Early Harvest Programme boosted ASEAN's exports of tropical produce to China, the increased Chinese export of temperate produce and manufactured goods to ASEAN countries caused resentment among local producers and again stirred up fears of Chinese domination (Bernardino 2004; Wattanapruttipaisan 2003).

4. China's response to the global financial crisis

Beijing has been praised by the international community for its swiftness to inject stimuli into the national economy, which is regarded as indirectly beneficial for other countries because of its demand for goods and commodities. The Chinese government also prides itself on its decisiveness in adopting such measures, which indeed have had immediate positive effects on GDP growth. China's swiftness is often contrasted with American indecisiveness as Washington had a lot of trouble ensuring the stimulus packages could be approved by the Congress, and uncertainty in such a process has led to market fluctuations.

However, it is worth examining whether, apart from the ability to spend money quickly, money has been distributed in a 'scientific' way in China and whether it contributes to 'scientific development', a catchphrase in China's current development strategy. Even though the long-term impacts of the measures adopted by the Chinese government remain to be seen, three problems in China's responses to the global financial crises are highlighted here as a cautionary note to the Beijing Consensus type of decision-making institution and development strategy: the concentration of distributional power and the resultant irrational decisions, the bias towards state-owned enterprises, and continued reliance on labour-intensive manufacturing and export.

4.1. Concentration of distributional power

The power to supply stimulus funding has been concentrated in the hands of very few actors. At the national level, the distributional power is designated to the National Development and Reform Commission (NDRC) and Ministry of Finance (MOF), supported by industry-line ministries. Concentration of power contributed to the swiftness of decision-making and reduced coordination problems, of which Beijing is proud, but such concentration also has far-reaching implications and risks for China's political economy.

After two attempts at government reform to reduce its power, the role of NDRC in Chinese domestic politics is reinforced thanks to the global crisis as it assumed the 'headquarters' position in government crisis response. The NDRC has inherited a conservative position on reform and opening from its former body, the State Planning Commission. During Premier Zhu Rongji's institutional reforms in 1998 and 2003, not only were parts of the State Planning Commission's institutions abolished to reduce the planning element of the state's role in the economy, but also the newly formed NDRC became largely a research and advisory agency to the central government. However, the NDRC has enjoyed increased power in domestic politics under the Hu-Wen leadership. As domestic stability and development problems became increasingly prominent in particular because of simplistic (*cufang*) liberalization, a more heavy-handed approach has been adopted by the government to intervene in the domestic economy. A more aggressive industrial policy is also adopted to promote national champions in global competition. NDRC is a central agency to carry out such macro-economic 'control' (*tiaokong*). It oversees national macro-economic, energy, price, industrial and investment policies amongst others. Because of the heavy control component in its portfolio and its inheritance from its former body, the NDRC represents the visible hand of planning in China's economic governance. Other government agencies call the NDRC a 'small state council' or a super-ministry, because it has departments matching every sector of the economy and holds a higher political position than the ministries.

The concentration of power in the NDRC reached such a level that problems of lack of capacity there and resentment among other agencies started to surface. It was also obvious that China lacked a clear or coherent industrial policy, although it implicitly resides in the NDRC. An important task in the 2008 government 'big ministry' restructuring was to reduce the responsibilities of the NDRC through diverting part of its power to other agencies. The Ministry of Industry and Information Technology (MIIT) was established by adding more 'industrial policy responsibility' to the former Ministry of Information Industry. The State-owned Assets Supervision and

Administration Commission (SASAC) also became more assertive over its power to regulate state-owned enterprises (SOEs).

However, with the onset of the financial crisis, the NDRC assumed paramount power again over the national economy. *The Review of the National Development Plan 2008* and *Development Plan 2009* were drafted by the NDRC, which included the distribution of the RMB 4 trillion stimulus package. The content of the package will be discussed later, but it was obvious that the distribution was decided without wide consultation. An official from a municipal government in Henan province said that the NDRC was pushing local governments to come up with projects to submit for approval, in contrast to the cautious, slow process of vetting investment applications earlier (Liao 2009). At the end of 2008, in order to compete for the first batch of RMB 100 billion, local officials occupied all the hotels near the NDRC. In order to dispatch funds quickly, the NDRC also approved many applications that had been shelved earlier – the quality of those applications then is in question (author's interview, Beijing, 2009). There have been calls to publicize more detailed information about projects funded by the RMB 4 trillion, and problems with its usage have been reported sporadically (Wei 2009).

A lot of money and discretion were also granted to local governments and state banks. The stimulus packages were distributed to provincial governments, to be used in combination with provincial funding for supporting local projects. The central government also distributed 200 billion local government bonds, which may exacerbate the problem of local government debt. State commercial banks at various levels received administrative orders to fulfil quotas for giving out loans within a short time. In the first quarter of 2009, bank loans already reached 4.58 trillion yuan, mostly on infrastructure, public projects and mergers between SOEs, although part of it is also spent on agriculture, innovation and consumer loans (excluding houses) (Sun and Xi 2009). Such a rapid and particularistic distribution increases the possibility of corruption and bad loans. Coastal provinces like Guangdong complained that the first two batches of 100 and 130 billion yuan were heavily tilted towards middle and western regions although coastal areas were most severely hit by the crisis (Su 2009). It was also reported that local governments might not be able to provide the complementary investment needed for the RMB 4 trillion package: RMB 600 billion was needed but an estimated RMB 300 billion was available. However, local governments tried to match the state funding, not least because NDRC made it clear that for the first batch of RMB 100 billion investment, if a local government could not provide complementary funding, its future investment from the central government would be reduced. The two main instruments used by local governments to obtain funding are borrowing from banks and renting out land. Some local governments also set up investment companies for big projects with managers appointed by the Organization Department of the Party, evaluated by the local SASAC, funded by local finance, and projects approved through local NDRCs. Without adequate supervision after the approval of funding, the government bonds could be used first to pay salaries, build houses and buy cars, before they finally go to projects, a similar practice to how the stimulus was dispatched after the Asian financial crisis (Xing 2009).

With the discretionary power at all levels of government and banks, China's overseas investment, after a period of caution because of previous unwise decisions and host country resistance, is again encouraged to tap into various countries with a higher profile, causing more concerns in other countries and backlashes of economic nationalism. The Chinese way of obtaining natural resources through upstream long-term contracts and continued demand of raw materials have contributed to international price hikes of commodities such as iron ore and copper, which most Chinese importers have to absorb and in turn have added to the costs of Chinese producers and consumers. Although Chinese private carmaker Geely successfully acquired Volvo, the acquisition of Norwegian Elkem by the Chinese state-owned Bluestar has caused concern about the loss of leading technology to China. The China Investment Corporation (CIC), a sovereign wealth fund, and the planned China Investment Corporation II under SASAC are expected to be active in conducting overseas investment, but their capacity to make wise business decisions remain to be seen. For example, the CIC has received wide domestic criticism for huge losses in three major investments in Blackstone, Morgan Stanley and the American Reserve Primary Fund.

Compared with the NDRC, SASAC and MIIT, MOFCOM is a more liberal pocket within the Chinese government, but it cannot do much in a protectionist international environment and under domestic pressure to ensure GDP growth. MOFCOM adopted measures to boost exports, such as resuming export tax rebates on some labour-intensive products that China has traditional comparative advantage in and had been trying to gradually move away from. Such measures are easily subject to international criticism for being protectionist or mercantilist. MOFCOM, with the help of industrial associations, is also busy fighting trade wars, in the form of both responding to anti-dumping allegations and defending restrictions on Chinese exports of raw materials. Certainly, the MOFCOM participates in WTO negotiations, but its room for concession is much constrained by domestic economic and political conditions. In particular, a large number of migrant workers lost their jobs at manufacturing factories in coastal areas and were forced to return to their farmland, some of which no longer existed because of land development and government appropriation. China's negotiations on the WTO Government Procurement Agreement (GPA) is underway, but the China–EU Chamber of Commerce and some of the world's largest companies, including General Electric, Siemens and BASF, have recently complained that China preferred domestic bidders and the investment environment in China in general (Li 2009; Anderlini 2010). Although China is not yet a member of the GPA while the US is, both countries' initiative to encourage the purchase of domestic products suggest that nationalism speaks louder than internationalism.

In short, the distributional power in China's crisis response was concentrated in the hands of a few actors, in particular the NDRC, MIIT and SASAC, which are known for having a cautious attitude towards reform and liberalization. Transparency and consultation are lacking in the distribution and usage of the funds at state and local levels of the government. It is questionable whether such decision-making could be scientific, as the funding is likely to favour a few actors who lobby intensively, to use state resources on projects without enough scrutiny, and to increase the element of planning in the domestic economy.

4.2. Bias towards state-owned enterprises and labour-intensive manufacturing

State-owned enterprises are the major beneficiaries of the stimulus packages. The stimulus plans for ten industries (automotive, steel, non-ferrous metals, textile, equipment and machinery manufacturing, ship manufacturing, information, light manufacturing, petro-chemicals and logistics) have a clear bias towards heavy industries and labour-intensive industries. Statistics from the first quarter of 2009 show that RMB 4.58 trillion of bank loans have gone to the 'second industries' (26.8% increase, cf. 85%, 29% for first and third industries) like real estate, electrical appliances, coal, concrete, metals, port and machinery, which are dominated by SOEs. Each of the industrial stimulus plans was drafted by the NDRC, supported by MIIT, business associations and representatives of big enterprises in the industry. Implementation of the plans are usually monitored by the NDRC and MIIT. In several of them (automotive, shipbuilding, electronics, IT), expansion of SOEs through mergers or alliances is encouraged (e.g. with tax breaks). For example, the drafting group for the shipbuilding industry stimulus plan decided that if small companies could not change businesses or merge with big companies, they had to go bankrupt. Several industry-line ministries jointly requested the State Council to set up an export credit guarantee company at the CIC to help the financing of export-oriented SOEs.

The SASAC is supposed to regulate SOEs and is in charge of SOE reform towards market economy standards. In practice, however, the role of SASAC has always been unclear, particularly whether it is a shareholder, regulator or manager. It is therefore sometimes called 'the great butler of SOEs'. The SASAC held a meeting in January 2009 to set the annual profit targets for state SOEs as a measurement of the performance of their managers, and the Enterprise State Asset Law came into force on 1 May 2009, with the ambition of clarifying and strengthening the role of the SASAC as an investor and asset manager. Despite these measures, the portfolio of SASAC remains unclear. The new law leaves room for several industries to retain a state monopoly, but still it has already met with arguments from enterprises and their line ministries about how to decide the budget of SOEs. SASAC has been investigating the problem of excessive expansion by SOEs since mid 2008, but the government's crisis response clearly encourages expansion of SOEs. Instead of further market reforms, SASAC is authorized by the State Council to design measures to rescue the SOEs with huge losses in the form of cash or the SOEs being taken over by the State Asset Management Corporation. Although the official rhetoric mentioned support for small and medium enterprises (SMEs), reports continue to show the difficulty that SMEs have in obtaining loans. For example, RMB 1.6 trillion went to the railway system but the profitable segments were taken over by SOEs under the Ministry of Railways, leaving small or private enterprises with no incentive to invest (R. Wang 2009).

In short, the stimulus packages strengthened the role of heavy industries, the big SOEs as well as their line ministries in the domestic political economy. The cultivation of SOEs as monopolies runs the risk of creating rents, discouraging innovation as well as foreign investment. And as the power of monopolies grows, it would become more difficult for the state to regulate SOEs or to pursue more balanced development.

4.3. Continued reliance on labour-intensive manufacturing and export

The stimulus packages represent a setback in China's effort to upgrade the industrial structure. The measures encourage China's traditional comparative advantage in labour-intensive sectors and promotes exports despite its rhetoric over stimulating domestic demand. Even though the development model that relies heavily on export of cheap manufacturing goods has created many jobs and accumulated huge foreign reserves for China, the Chinese government has realized many drawbacks of this model. Chinese leaders have started to emphasize sustainable, balanced and 'scientific' development, with an ambition of climbing up the value chain and gradually moving sunset industries out of China.

However, the global financial crisis set the clock back for several labour-intensive sectors. The decision to halt the appreciation of RMB in mid 2008 was one measure to support exports. China also resumed tax rebates for the export of labour-intensive products. The stimulus plan for the textile industry 2009–2011 that came out in April 2009 includes stabilizing export markets, increasing export tax rebates and exploring multiple markets. In another sector that has over-capacity problems, China started a rural movement – a four-year 'electronic appliances going to the countryside movement'. It is led by MOF, MOFCOM and MIIT and uses administrative measures to push up local consumption. The brands being promoted in this movement were chosen from a domestic bid to the China Electronics Import and Export Corporation. Just as the rural movements are Chinese in character, local government measures often follow old Chinese ways of fulfilling tasks. For example, some local governments even imposed quotas for lower-level government units to fulfil. In some places, the sales of electronic appliances did rise because of reduced prices, but there is also evidence that some farmers regard this movement as another trick of the government to try to get money out of their pockets.

The problem of over-capacity was exacerbated as a result of the stimulus packages. For instance, as a result of the support of construction and infrastructure in the RMB 4 trillion stimulus package and the industrial plans for automotive, steel, machinery and shipbuilding, investment in steel production, which hit RMB 140.5 billion in the first half of 2009, was expected to lift the annual capacity to more than 700m tons, compared with domestic demand of about 500 m tons in 2008 (Xinjingbao 2009). At the same time, as mentioned earlier, international iron ore prices rose due to Chinese imports. Domestic overcapacity and reduced demand for steel products has led to the fall of the steel price and bankruptcy of a large number of factories, for instance in Hebei and Jiangsu provinces. The problem of over-capacity became so severe that the State Council made a statement in September 2009 that highly polluting sectors including steel, coke, cement and plate glass must cut capacity, while silicon and wind power producers should pursue more orderly development. With more state components in the economy, the government may be able to strengthen its regulation over SOEs and to cultivate national champions to become global competitors, as well as to monitor risky behaviour such as investment in financial derivatives. However, the effect of such regulations is limited. Not only private companies but also SOEs continue to pursue their own economic interests and strategies regardless of government criticism.

A crucial task of the crisis response was to stimulate domestic demand. However, the original plan for the RMB 4 trillion stimulus package was criticized for not spending enough on social welfare; instead, it focused heavily on the construction of schools and hospitals in this policy area. The expenditure on social welfare was increased in the revised version of the RMB 4 trillion plan, which reflects the influence of public opinion on state policy. The 2009 budget increased the spending on health, education and social insurance by 20%, but the share only increased 0.9%, to 7.1% (cf. 15–30% in developed countries). The government lifted the restraints on residency in Beijing and Shanghai for new university graduates, and ordered some SOEs to hire a certain number of university graduates, but unemployment continues to be a serious problem in China and there is little unemployment subsidy. Stimulating domestic demand in China seems to remain a long-term, challenging task. A central source of China's international power, a huge domestic market, may become merely an illusion.

5. Discussion: implications for the 'responsible great power' diplomacy

Undoubtedly, China seeks the image and status of a 'responsible great power', with its moral and material superiority attributed to the Beijing Consensus or the China Model. However, the above analysis shows that China's development strategy contains significant problems and risks. They not only render the model difficult and even dangerous to copy by other developing countries, but also may compromise China's ideational and material superiority if those problems become serious. As China's response to the global financial crisis shows, it is already constrained by domestic political and economic conditions in providing public goods or showing great power style to smaller countries in Asia or elsewhere.

In trade, measures that promote labour-intensive manufacturing goods are resumed as mentioned earlier, and this intensifies competition with other Asian and developing countries. Reduced exports means large numbers of laid-off workers and possibly social unrest, something Beijing can ill afford. For Chinese leaders, domestic stability is the greatest concern; in other words, a 'harmonious society' precedes a 'harmonious world'. In its pursuit of multiple export markets, China has contributed much more to the creation of bilateral and regional institutions than to the WTO despite widespread criticism that FTAs have spaghetti bowl or noodle bowl effects on world trade. Just as US bilateralism in the 1990s launched a second wave of FTAs, Chinese activism seems to have kickstarted another domino effect. China is still reluctant to accept a multilateral regional trade regime in Northeast Asia or East Asia, largely because of political rivalry with Japan, but also because of concern over potential competition from the products and services of developed Asian countries. At the WTO, China has kept a tough position since its entry, in particular over agriculture, services and intellectual property rights (IPRs). China criticises major Western countries for protectionism during the global financial crisis, but it does not wish to be labelled as the leader of developing countries because 'the distribution of interests at the WTO are very complex and changeable' (author's interview with MOFCOM officials, Beijing, May 2006, July 2009). China has successfully created a category of 'newly accessed members' at the WTO to avoid many further concessions. In finance, the global financial crisis has brought China new opportunities to demonstrate great power style and the superiority of the China Model. In a significant step in May 2009, China agreed to contribute the same amount of money as Japan (US$38.4 billion each) to the expansion of the Multilateralization of the Chiang Mai Initiative (CMIM) reserve pool in May 2009. China also signed bilateral swap arrangements from December 2008 to March 2009 with South Korea, Hong Kong, Malaysia, Belarus, Indonesia and Argentina worth a total of RMB 650 billion. It should be noted that BSAs are a shallow form of financial cooperation and carry low risk for the potential lender. For deeper and riskier forms of financial cooperation, such as exchange rate coordination, China has lacked enthusiasm due to its closed capital account, 'managed floating' exchange rate policy and lack of confidence in its financial institutions. China remains resistant to the idea of an Asian currency and reluctant to build an independent surveillance mechanism in East Asia. However, China has started promoting the usage of RMB in its neighbouring countries and some other developing countries that have close trade ties with China. Apart from the stabilising effect on trade, those measures are designed as gradual steps towards the internationalization of RMB, because China recognises seigniorage as a source of international power, and presages RMB to be one of the international reserve currencies. However, with the risk of insolvency at local governments and state commercial banks, financial liberalization and thus China's role as lender of last resort are still a long way off.

At global financial institutions, China used the opportunity of the global financial crisis to call for an increase of voice from developing countries and prides itself on the rise of the G20 against the G7. At the same time, China is careful not to be burdened by the 'China responsibility' discourse with 'unduly high or even blind expectations'. A researcher at MOFCOM even announced that the China responsibility discourse was just another version of the China threat rhetoric, and China would refuse responsibilities imposed by others for such titles as a surplus country, a debtor country, a savings nation, a big energy consumer or a big CO_2 emissions country (Xinhua 2010). It is not hard to understand China's caution given signals of looming domestic economic problems.

In summary, the lesson that China learned from the Asian financial crisis was not the importance of liberalization but prudence or conservativeness, which despite serving as a shield in the global financial crisis, sustains problems in the long term. Since the Asian financial crisis, China's obsession with foreign reserves accumulation and the pursuit of political influence have overshadowed the increasing dependence on the US market, now causing China dilemmas in both development and diplomatic strategies towards developing countries. The Beijing Consensus type of decision-making may be faster than democratic processes, but it may also go against the principle of 'scientific decision' or 'balanced development' as proposed by the Chinese leadership. A prominent feature of China's response to the crisis is a bias towards state-owned enterprises and the public sector, which runs the risk of monopoly, over-capacity, inequality, the regulators being 'captured' by industrial interests and protectionism. The status of a responsible great power either in the region or in the world remains Beijing's aspiration, still far from reality.

Acknowledgements

The author thanks Kjeld Erik Brødsgaard, Ari Kokko, Anthony D'Costa, Anna Leander, Peter Nolan, Sanjay Peters, Jonas Parello-Presner and anonymous reviewers for their comments on earlier drafts.

References

Amsden, A. H. (2001) *The Rise of 'The Rest': Challenges to the West from Late Industrializing Economies*, Oxford: Oxford University Press.

Anderlini, J. (2010) 'China's partners set to reject trade plan', *Financial Times*, 19 July.

Baek, S.-W. (2005) 'Does China follow "the East Asian development model"?', *Journal of Contemporary Asia* 35(4): 485–98.

Beeson, M. (2009) 'Developmental states in East Asia: a comparison of the Japanese and Chinese experiences', *Asia Perspective* 33(2): 5–39.

Bernardino, N. Y. (2004) 'The ASEAN–China free trade area: issues and prospects', *Asia Pacific Network on Food Sovereignty Regional Workshop Papers*, 6–9 November.

Breslin, S. (1999) 'The politics of Chinese trade and the Asian financial crises: questioning the wisdom of export-led growth', *Third World Quarterly* 20(6): 1179–99.

Breslin, S. (2003) 'Paradigm shifts and time-lags? The politics of financial reform in the People's Republic of China', *Asian Business and Management* 2(1): 143–66.

Breslin, S. (2007) *China and the Global Political Economy*, New York: Palgrave Macmillan.

Fan, Gang (1999) 'Quanqiuhua zhong de Bupingdeng Wenti: Yazhou Jinrong Weiji de Jiaoxun ji Zhengce Hanyi' [Inequality in globalization: lessons from the Asian financial crisis and policy implications], *Guoji Jingji Pinglun* [*International Economic Review*] 3: 41–44.

Fan, Gang (2010) 'Getting economic recipe right', *China Daily*, 2 July, p. 8.

Feng, H. (2006) *The Politics of China's Accession to the World Trade Organisation: The Dragon Goes Global*, London and New York: Routledge.

Gill, B. and Huang, Y. (2006) 'Sources and limits of Chinese "soft power"', *Survival* 48(2): 17–36.

He, F. (2007) 'China's economic reform: success, problems and challenges', *EABER Working Paper 19*, Tokyo: East Asian Bureau of Economic Research.

Hellman, J. S. (1998) 'Winners take all: the politics of partial reform in postcommunist transitions', *World Politics* 50(2): 203–34.

Higgott, R. (1998) 'The Asian economic crisis: a study in the politics of resentment', *New Political Economy* 3(3): 333–56.

Kennedy, S. (2010) 'The myth of the Beijing Consensus', *Journal of Contemporary China* 19(65): 461–77.

Kerr, D. (2007) 'Has China abandoned self-reliance?', *Review of International Political Economy* 14(1): 77–104.

Kindleberger, C. (1975) *The World in Depression: 1929–1939*, Berkeley: University of California Press.

Kroeber, A. (2008) 'Rising China and the liberal West', *China Economic Quarterly* 12(1): 29–44.

Kupchan, C. A. (1998) 'After Pax Americana: benign power, regional integration, and the sources of a stable multipolarity', *International Security* 23(2): 40–79.

Kurlantzick, J. (2007) *Charm Offensive: How China's Soft Power Is Transforming the World*, New Haven, CT: Yale University Press.

Li, Qiang (2009) 'Fagaiwei huiying 4 wanyi caigou paiwai zhize: cheng guohuo zao qishi' [NDRC responds to 4 trillion procurement excludes foreign products: saying domestic products are discriminated against], *Xinwen Chenbao* [*News Morning*], 2 June.

Liao, Haiqing (2009) 'The Henan sample of the 4 trillion cake distribution' [siwanyi qiedangao de henan yangben], Nan Feng Chuang [*South Wind Window*], 19 March, accessed at http://blog.sina.com.cn/s/blog_4c9474490100crdf.html~type=v5_one&label=rela_nextarticle.

Liaowang (2004) 'Zhongguo tisheng ruanshili: "beijing gongshi" qudai "huashengdun gongshi"' [China enhances soft power: 'Beijing Consensus' replaces 'Washington Consensus'], 13 June, accessed at http://news.xinhuanet.com/newscenter/2004-06/13/content_1522884.htm. Accessed 25 June 2011.

Noble, G. W. and Ravenhill, J. (2000) 'The good, the bad and the ugly? Korea, Taiwan and the Asian financial crisis', in G. W. Noble and J. Ravenhill (eds) *The Asian Financial Crisis and the Architecture of Global Finance*, Cambridge: Cambridge University Press, pp. 80–107.

Rachman, G. (2008) 'Illiberal capitalism: Russia and China chart their own course', *Financial Times*, 8 January.

Ramo, J. C. (2004) *The Beijing Consensus*, London: Foreign Policy Centre.

Ravenhill, J. (2006) 'Is China an economic threat to Southeast Asia?', *Asian Survey* 46(5): 653–74.

Renmin Luntan (2009) 'Xifang sanda yuyan rentongdu diaocha' [Survey on the agreement with the West's three predictions], 26 March.

Schubert, G. (2008) 'One-party rule and the question of legitimacy in contemporary China: preliminary thoughts on setting up a new research agenda', *Journal of Contemporary China* 17(54): 191–204.

Steinfeld, E. (2008) 'Embrace of capitalism: China ten years after the Asian financial crisis', in A. Macintyre, T. J. Pempel and J. Ravenhill (eds) *Crisis as Catalyst: Asia's Dynamic Political Economy*, Ithaca, NY: Cornell University Press, pp. 183–205.

Stubbs, R. (2005) *Rethinking Asia's Economic Miracle*, Basingstoke: Palgrave.

Su, Yongtong (2009) '09 caizheng yusuan fenpei jiemi: sanda minsheng zhichu jin tigao 0.9%' [09 fiscal budget distribution: three major welfare expense only increases 0.9%], *Nanfang Zhoumo* [*Southern Weekend*], 12 March.

Sun, Jianfang and Xi, Si (2009) 'Jigou diaoyan xianshi 4 wanyi xindai zijin zhengliuru channeng guosheng hangye' [Institution's Research show 4 trillion credit is flowing into over-capacity sectors], *Jingji Guancha Bao* [*Economic Watch*], 24 April.

Sun, Jie (2007) 'Shenhua Yazhou Jinrong Hezuo de Tujing: Riben de Zuoyong he Yingxiang' [Ways to deepen Asian financial cooperation: Japan's role and influence], *Shijie Jingji yu Zhengzhi* [*World Economy and Politics*] 5: 59–66.

Teo, E. C. C. (2004) 'Asian security and the reemergence of China's tributary system', *China Brief* 4(18), Washington DC: Jamestown Foundation, 16 September.

Terry, E. (2002) *How Asia Got Rich: Japan, China, and the Asian Miracle*, Armonk, NY: M. E. Sharpe.

The Economist (2008) 'China's fiscal stimulus: Dr Keynes's Chinese patient', 13 November.

Wang, Mengkui (1998) 'Yazhou Jinrong Weiji yu Zhongguo' [Asian financial crisis and China], *Qiushi* [*Seeking Truth*] 21:9.

Wang, Rengui (2009) 'Guojia 4 wanyi duo guanzhu guoqi, minying fazhan zaoyu 5 da pingjing' [government's 4 trillion goes mostly to SOEs, private companies face 5 bottlenecks], *Liaowang*, 2 December.

Wang, Y. (1998) 'Causes, impacts of the Asian financial crisis and China's measures: a summary of the symposium "Asian Financial Crisis: Views from China and the US" conference', *Meiguo Yanjiu* [*American Studies*] 3: 147–52.

Wattanapruttipaisan, T. (2003) 'ASEAN–China free trade area: advantages, challenges, and implications for the newer ASEAN member countries', *ASEAN Economic Bulletin* 20(1): 31–48.

Wei, Zhenni (2009) '4 trillion investment needs transparent supervision' [4wanyi yuan touzi qidai yangguang jianguan], *Zhongguo chanjing xinwen* [*China Industry and Economy News*], 1 June, accessed at http://finance.ifeng.com/news/hgjj/20090531/723243.shtml.

World Bank (1993) *The East Asian Miracle: Economic Growth and Public Policy* (World Bank Policy Research Reports), New York: Oxford University Press.

Xiao, Qi (2006) 'Ziben Xiangmu Kaifang yu Jinrong Anquan' [Capital account liberalization and financial security], *Jinrong Jiaoxue yu Yanjiu* [*Finance Education and Studies*] 3: 11–13, 25.

Xinjingbao (2009) 'Woguo tiekuangshi kucunliang chao yidun' [Iron ore storage in our country exceeds 100 million tons], 14 May.

Xinhua News Agency (2010) 'Zhuanjia bochi zhongguo jingji zerenlun' [Expert refutes China responsibility discourse], 15 August, accessed at http://www.china.com.cn/economic/txt/2010-08/16/content_20714847.htm.

Xing, Shaowen (2009) '2000 yi difangzhai yinren guanzhu: xuduo difang zhengfu yi zhaitai gaozhu' [200 billion local debt attracts concern: many local governments are heavily indebted], *Nan Feng Chuang* [*South Wind Window*], 17 March.

Yao, Y. (2010) 'The end of the Beijing Consensus: can China's model of authoritarian growth survive?', *Foreign Affairs*, 2 February.

Yu, Yongding (2007) 'Yazhou Jinrong Weiji 10 Zhounian he Zhongguo Jingji' [10th anniversary of Asian financial crisis and Chinese economy], *Guoji Jinrong Yanjiu* [*International Financial Studies*] 8: 1–13.

Zhong, Wei (2008) '1~3 niannei, Naxie Yinsu Keneng Yingxiang Woguo Jinrong Wending' [Within 1–3 years, which factors may affect China's financial stability], *Diyi Caijing Ribao* [*First Finance Daily*], 5 May.

Zhou, Xiaochuan (2009) 'Reform the international monetary system', 23 March, accessed at http://www.pbc.gov.cn/english/detail.asp?col=6500&id=178.

Zoellick, R. B. (2005) 'Whither China: from membership to responsibility?', excerpts of the remarks to the National Committee on the United States and China Relations, presented in New York City, 21 September, accessed at http://www.disam.dsca.mil/pubs/INDEXES/Vol%2028_2/Zoellick.pdf.

Crisis dynamics and regionalism: East Asia in comparative perspective

Mark Beeson

Abstract This paper compares the current global financial crisis with the one that struck East Asia a little more than a decade ago. The analysis reveals some striking and surprising differences between the two periods. Whereas the first crisis had a catalytic impact on Asian regionalism this one may not. Despite East Asia generally and China in particular seeming to emerge stronger relative to the US from the current crisis, the impact of the second crisis on Europe reminds us that there is nothing inevitable about the course of regional integration. Not only are Europe's economic problems likely to diminish whatever enthusiasm there was for initiatives such as a common currency in Asia, but China may also find itself increasingly playing a global rather than a regional role. In short, crises can have very different impacts and provide an important insight into the interconnected dynamics of regional and global processes.

Mark Beeson is Winthrop Professor of Political Science and International Studies at the University of Western Australia. Before joining UWA at the beginning of 2010, he taught at the universities of Murdoch, Griffith, Queensland, York (UK) and Birmingham, where he was also head of department. Professor Beeson's work is centred on the politics, economics and security of the broadly conceived Asia-Pacific region. He is the author of more than 100 journal articles and book chapters, as well as numerous other publications. His latest books include *Institutions of the Asia-Pacific: ASEAN, APEC and Beyond* (Routledge, 2009), *Securing Southeast Asia: The Politics of Security Sector Reform* (with Alex Bellamy, Routledge, 2008), *Regionalism and Globalization in East Asia: Politics, Security and Economic Development* (Palgrave, 2007), and the recently published edited collection *Issues in 21st Century World Politics* (with Nick Bisley, Palgrave, 2010).

Introduction

What a difference a decade makes. During 1997–98, East Asia was at the epicentre of a major crisis that seemed to spell the end of the 'Asian miracle', and which threatened to go global. With its currencies in freefall and economic activity – to say nothing of its banks and governments – collapsing, the region became synonymous with crony capitalism and regime change. Governments fell and so did economic models. Claims about the superiority of Asia's economies and values suddenly looked rather threadbare – especially when the International Monetary Fund took the opportunity to put the 'Asian model' to the rhetorical sword (Hall 2003). Put crudely, and at the risk of mixing metaphors, 'Asia' was seemingly on the skids and being force-fed an unpalatable diet of neoliberal humble pie. Now, little more than ten years later, the region is one of the few bright spots in the global economy and it is the 'Anglo-American model' that is in need of resuscitation and subject to withering retrospective criticism (Altman 2009).

How did this transformation come about in such a remarkably short period of time? In order to answer this question, I place the two crises in comparative perspective and consider their respective dynamics, as well as their surprising interconnections. Seen in a longer time frame, one of the most striking features of the second crisis (which has yet to show any sign of definitively abating at the time of writing), is how deeply connected it is to the first episode that was manifest primarily in East Asia. Ironically enough, the response of East Asian governments to the first crisis helped create the preconditions for the second: East Asian savings and trade surpluses ultimately allowed Americans to 'live beyond their means' as consumers and the government borrowed from Asia's seemingly limitless reserves. They also provided the fuel for an explosion of financial innovation as Wall Street found ever more exotic ways to recycle huge inflows of capital (Tett 2009).

The consequences of over-reliance on inadequately regulated financial sectors for countries such as the US and Britain have become painfully apparent. Such failings are, however, arguably symptomatic of more fundamental transformations in both the way we think about economic governance and about underlying structural change in the international economy. In both cases, East Asia seems likely to be the long-term beneficiary of recent events in absolute and relative terms: not only has the material position of the East Asian region been enhanced, but it is not inconceivable that the region's famously 'statist' orientation to economic management is likely to become more influential (Zhao 2010). There are two other major comparative points that emerge from the following analysis. One is about the nature of regions and regional dynamics: whereas the first crisis of globalisation provided a major boost to regional integration in East Asia, the current crisis is having precisely the opposite effect in Europe. The second is about the relative standing of China and the US: in the first crisis China was a relative bystander and the US was able to impose a reformist agenda on a largely unenthusiastic East Asian region. In the second, the US is a notably diminished force and it is China that is increasingly looked to as the catalyst for economic recovery. Although the principal focus in what follows is on East Asia, a comparative focus tells us something important about both the practical prospects for Europe and East Asia, as well as sharpening our understanding of the nature of regional processes. In what follows, therefore, I first briefly revisit the two global crises, before drawing out and analysing their comparative dynamics and significance.

The first crisis of globalisation

It is easy to see why the East Asian crisis was labelled the first crisis of globalisation (Higgott 2000: 262). In many ways this was an accurate description, because one of its key characteristics was the way that it spread relentlessly, first within East Asia itself, and subsequently to Russia, Latin America and even the US itself. Indeed, when the Federal Reserve decided to orchestrate a bail-out of the failed hedge fund Long-Term Capital Management (LTCM) it was a harbinger of the current crisis, both in terms of its causes and its subsequent management.[1] With the benefit of hindsight, it is clear that policymakers in the US and elsewhere missed an important warning sign and opportunity for preventative regulatory intervention when LTCM went under. It is testimony to the then dominance of American finance capital, the influence of free market ideology, and the continuing belief in the superiority of Anglo-American capitalism that such warnings went unheeded.[2]

There are a number of crucial differences between the earlier crisis and the current one which help to explain the way the US was affected and responded. On the one hand, the impact of the crisis on the US was relatively limited and containable: despite the scale of the rescue bid organised by the Federal Reserve in 1998, it is dwarfed by the current crisis. On the other hand, the East Asian crisis was seen by American policymakers in particular as an essentially *regional* problem. Indeed, East Asia's problems were seen as a consequence and indictment of 'crony capitalism', a vindication of the rectitude and superiority of Anglo-American forms of political and economic organisation, and an opportunity to encourage the further opening up of the entire East Asian region (Chang 2000). In retrospect, of course, it is plain that such hubris was misplaced and such ambitions ill-conceived. It is also clear that a real opportunity to impose genuine reform on the 'international financial architecture' was missed (Armijo 2001). Had such reforms been undertaken it is entirely possible that the current crisis would have been much less severe, more manageable and less damaging.

Before considering the impact of the current turmoil in any detail, however, it is important to remind ourselves of the way in which 'East Asia's' crisis unfolded as it generated institutional initiatives at the regional level that remain influential, important, and which present a striking contrast to the impact of the current crisis. Perhaps the key long-term consequence of the first crisis was to change the way policymakers in East Asia thought about 'globalisation' and the benefits to be obtained from deeper integration into the wider international economy (Grimes 2009). Although the financial sector played a critical and destabilising role in both crises, what is strikingly different and of greatest potential long-term significance has been the nature of regional responses.

East Asia and monetary regionalism

To understand what has driven cooperation in the financial sector thus far in East Asia, we need to place the region's crisis in its specific geopolitical context. The key issue in this regard was the belated recognition that not only did 'globalisation' present threats as well as opportunities, but it was a process that was driven by the US and the powerful international institutions created under the auspices of American hegemony. The creation and operation of the so-called Bretton Woods institutions – the IMF, the World Bank and the World Trade Organization – was intentionally designed to maintain an 'open', liberal, increasingly integrated global economy (Beeson 2006). Whatever we may think about the actual operations of these institutions, there is little doubt that they have been highly successful in this mission to this point. It is also evident that the remarkable economic transformation that has occurred in East Asia owes much to the opportunities this open economic order presented. Indeed, the rapid rise of China is a powerful reminder of the potential benefits that flow from entry into this order and key institutions like the WTO which oversee its operation (Lardy 2002).

And yet for all the benefits that undoubtedly flowed from greater economic interdependence – not the least an underlying improvement in strategic relations – it is also clear that deeper financial integration and openness carries potentially enormous dangers. East Asia's vulnerability to forces over which it had limited control, particularly the massive, destabilising flows of highly mobile capital that wreaked such havoc during the first crisis, were the proverbial wake-up call for the region's political and economic elites (Beeson 2007). However, what was distinctive about the region's collective response to the crisis was that it is not simply a 'technical' question of redesigning the region's financial architecture. On the contrary, it also became evident that the crisis, its management and its aftermath had significant geopolitical consequences.

One of the most important aspects of the first crisis was the widely noted role of the IMF in managing its aftermath. The key issue in this context was not simply that the IMF's policies were judged to be inappropriate and misguided, but that they were actually designed to further the interests of external actors, primarily the US and 'Wall Street'. While this is an unsatisfactory way of attempting to describe a complex set of relations between the US government and financial sector actors domiciled in the US, it does capture something important and meaningful about what Jagdish Bhagwati (1998) famously described as the 'Wall St–Treasury complex'. The US's (then) powerful financial sector had a clear vested interest in expanding its geographical reach; the increased size of the financial sector in the US meant that it also had a greater and greater influence on the Bush administration's domestic and foreign policy (Panitch and Gindin 2004). An agenda of economic liberalisation was consequently a prominent feature of the reform package promoted by the IMF in East Asia in the aftermath of the first crisis. If the US's response to the Asian crisis was a predictable and illuminating manifestation of its geopolitical weight at that time, the response of East Asia's putative great powers was equally revealing. Significantly, efforts by the Japanese to establish an Asian Monetary Fund with which to respond to the crisis were rapidly squashed by the US; Japan's continuing strategic subordination to the US meant that Japan's political leaders had little initial enthusiasm for a major disagreement with the principal guarantor of its security. What was most significant about this episode in retrospect, perhaps, was the recognition that Japan and the US had divergent interests and that Japan might actually benefit from constructing a distinctively 'East Asian' response to the crisis (Lee 2006). China's response to the crisis, although attracting less attention at the time, has ultimately proved to have been the most portentous. By not devaluing its currency at the height of the crisis, when the temptation to do so was immense and the damage to its own economic competitiveness was not inconsiderable, China won the gratitude of its neighbours and established itself as both a responsible and consequential regional power (Wang 2003).

The belated recognition on the part of East Asian political elites that they were vulnerable to politically motivated external pressures stimulated an interest in developing regional monetary mechanisms with which to manage future crises. The much-discussed Chiang-Mai initiative established in 2000, and related proposals to establish a regional bond market, are the most important expressions of this goal. The proposed currency swap arrangements in particular were a potentially crucial part of what has been described as an expanding process of 'monetary regionalism' in which cooperation between Asian states is becoming more institutionalised (Dieter 2008). The currency swap arrangements have received the most attention, and it is not hard to understand why: not only could such arrangements provide a degree of insulation and autonomy for the region in the event of any future crisis, but East Asia as a whole has the economic capacity to underwrite such arrangements. In other words, the financial sector provides a rationale for greater regional cooperation in an area where East Asia has the potential to turn rhetoric into reality.

Unsurprisingly, China and Japan are at the centre of the proposed currency swap mechanisms because they have the region's greatest foreign exchange reserves. However, it is noteworthy that despite the potential attractions of such a scheme in rendering the region less vulnerable to future crises – be they internally or externally driven – both China and Japan appear reluctant to make open-ended commitments to their impoverished neighbours, and have generally been happy for the IMF to oversee such arrangements (Ravenhill 2002). Despite being presented with an opportunity to provide regional leadership, both of East Asia's most important economic actors have seemed unwilling to take the initiative and thus far have been willing to abide by the status quo. As Heribert Dieter (2008: 496) points out, the rivalry between Japan and China is one of the key obstacles to cooperation in this area as it is in intra-regional political and strategic issues more generally. As a result, even in the area of financial sector reform where monetary regionalism has arguably made the most progress, initiatives have remained broadly supportive of the existing global financial arrangements (Grimes 2006: 357).

But even though the extent of cooperation within East Asia remained limited in the aftermath of the first crisis, the response of Asian states was in part responsible for planting the seeds of the next. The increased competitiveness generated by currency depreciations and a renewed export drive by the region's leaner and meaner manufacturing sector helped create the massive currency reserves which have become such a feature of the region's post-crisis defensive economic posture (*The Economist* 2010). It was these reserves which were recycled to the US and which would become such an integral part of the second crisis (Vasudevan 2009). Before considering how, it is important to spell out why the US was so willing to absorb them. Simply put, the long-run deterioration in the economic position of the US and its need to finance chronic deficits explains both its enthusiasm for international financial sector liberalisation and its reliance on continuing inflows of capital. As Robert Wade (2000, p. 107) puts it:

> The United States' reluctance to rein in external deficits, and its preference to finance them by creating debt that other countries accumulated as foreign exchange reserves ... produced a surge in world liquidity that eventually produced excess capacity and financial fragility worldwide. Both Japan's boom and bust and the later Asian miracle and bust were manifestations of the same systemic process.

The importance of the US economy and the absence of effective regional leadership in East Asia in the wake of the first crisis meant that this structural interdependence intensified. The US was able to exploit its structural power to shift the burden of adjustment caused by its own deteriorating economic circumstances onto other countries (Vermeiren 2010). Paradoxically, the US's massive liabilities actually became a source of leverage as other states became dependent on it as a market of last resort and an apparently safe investment haven. In the short term, at least, it was a relationship from which the US appeared to benefit and which US policymakers had little incentive to change. As a consequence, and despite the rhetoric about the need to reform the international financial architecture in the aftermath of the Asian crisis, little of substance changed (Soederberg 2001). Now, however, the entire international economic landscape has undergone something of a tectonic shift, and the potential – even the necessity – of fundamental reform is no longer as fanciful as it once seemed. Before considering what form this might take, and how this might impact on the East Asian region, it is important to spell out how the current crisis has unfolded and why it may lead to major changes at both the global and regional levels.

The second crisis of globalisation

There are two key initial points to make about the current crisis. First, this crisis cannot be dismissed as a 'regional' affair, even if some parts of the world have not been that badly affected. Equally importantly – and this is the second point – it is evident that this crisis had its origins in the liberal Anglo-American economies generally and in the US in particular (Foster and Magdoff 2009; Tett 2009). The dynamics and consequences of this crisis are proving to be entirely different as a result. In the first crisis the United States as the world's dominant political and economic power was able to encourage the adoption of specific reforms within those countries judged to have failed. On this occasion, the origins of global instability are to be found in the US itself. Yet despite being the principal source of the most recent crisis, the prospects for real reform are limited and the international financial system remains vulnerable to shifts in America's domestic politics.

In this context, there are serious doubts about the ability of successive US governments to recognise the depth of the crisis, much less adequately address it (Wolf 2009). The financial sector in the US has proved a powerful obstacle to reform and this has profound implications for the authority of the Obama administration. As the former chief economist of the IMF has pointed out:

> elite business interests – financiers, in the case of the U.S. – played a central role in creating the crisis, making ever-larger gambles, with the implicit backing of the government, until the inevitable collapse. More alarming, they are now using their influence to prevent precisely the sorts of reforms that are needed, and fast, to pull the economy out of its nosedive. The government seems helpless, or unwilling, to act against them. (Johnson 2009)

The possible inadequacy of the recently passed legislation designed to regulate Wall Street, which is widely thought to be too complex and riddled with loopholes to rein in the financial sector, is confirmation of this possibility (Reich 2010). What is of potentially even greater long-term significance is what the US's continuing economic problems mean for the wider international system. When the notional anchor of the international financial system has become a source of instability with an increasingly dysfunctional, polarised political system that struggles to institute much-needed reform (Jacobs and King 2009), other countries and regions are presented with an unprecedented challenge as they seek to recalibrate their domestic and foreign policies.

Sub-prime capitalism?

The current crisis has already been subjected to extensive analysis (Elliott and Atkinson 2008; Reinhart and Rogoff 2009), but it is worth briefly recapitulating its central dynamics as they continue to influence policy outcomes in the US and elsewhere. The principal features of the crisis are widely recognised and relatively uncontested: regulatory failures in the US and Britain meant that financial sector interests were given increasingly free rein to develop financial mechanisms, derivatives and innovations that generated enormous profits, but which did so by increasing, rather than diffusing systemic risk as their advocates had previously claimed (Crotty 2009). We now know that structured investment vehicles, collateralised debt obligations and the like were little more than exercises in paper-shuffling and self-delusion, but for a number of years they generated enormous profits for the banking sectors in Wall Street and the City of London. As a consequence, neither individual financial institutions nor the regulatory authorities in the US or Britain were motivated to question, much less effectively monitor, such activities. On the contrary, such financial sector innovations were actively encouraged and seen by the likes of Gordon Brown (2007) as critical to the long-term success of New York and London.

The predatory nature of Wall Street's relationship with the US domestic economy was revealed by the nature of the 'sub-prime crisis', in which the most vulnerable and impoverished of Americans were directly exploited by some of the most affluent and powerful (Blackburn 2008). As a consequence, there is now widespread outrage in the US about the nature of both the crisis itself and the reward and incentive structures that encouraged it. While there has been real momentum for reform in the US as a result, there is also widespread doubt about the Obama administration's ability to understand, much less decisively transform the underlying structures of American capitalism that allowed such excess and imbalances of power to occur in the first place (Wolf 2009). Nevertheless, it is plain that the sort of 'light touch', financial sector-driven neoliberalism that dominated the US and Britain for about two decades has been severely discredited, even if this has not translated into a fundamental shift in the balance of power between states and markets (Stephens 2010a).

The dynamics of this second crisis of globalisation consequently have both ideational and material effects that will shape political responses at multiple levels. At an ideational level, the demise of neoliberalism potentially opens up a political space for alternative models to replace the discredited Anglo-American orthodoxy, although given the pervasive influence of the bond markets this possibility should not be overstated – especially in Europe. Predictably enough, given the nature of the crisis and the worrying similarities between this crisis and the Great Depression, the ideas of John Maynard Keynes have enjoyed renewed popularity and salience. However, it is far from clear that the US will be able to play the same sort of role as it did in Keynes' time when it established the Bretton Woods institutions and provided the sort of 'hegemonic' leadership that some observers consider crucial for the maintenance of international economic stability (Kindleberger 1973). Not only has the US's own moral authority and influence been profoundly undermined by a crisis it is widely seen as having created, but it is not obvious what the best strategies or institutions may be for overcoming the current malaise. Such judgements are made more difficult because at the level of brute material reality the structural importance of the US is not as great as it once was; the diminished importance of the US economy raises serious questions about its continued ability to underpin America's broader leadership role and ambitions (Krugman 2009). After all, the US has failed leadership tests before, especially when it perceived national interests to be at stake (Beeson and Broome 2010).

Because governments in the US and the UK in particular considered that many of 'their' largest financial institutions were 'too big to fail', they received massive, taxpayer-funded bailouts. Such largesse has further weakened both economies and sparked an unresolved debate about the merits of, and/or constraints on, Keynesian-style stimulus packages. For sceptics, there are simply limits to how much money even the most powerful governments can promise, print or spend before a market-induced 'correction' is triggered (Ferguson 2010a). While the debate may not be resolved until the US and European economies are considered to have unambiguously recovered, its implications are already being felt in the world's financial markets. 'Sovereign debt crises' have become the latest focus of market attention, as doubts grow about the ability of the governments of Portugal, Ireland, Spain and especially Greece to meet their financial obligations (Wolf 2010).

Comparative crisis management

In the context of a discussion of the impact of financial crises on different parts of the world, there are a number of comparative points to be made. The most general point is that Europe's response to the crisis has been very different to Asia's earlier efforts and is likely to have very different implications for both Europe itself and perhaps the wider international economy as a consequence. Whatever the merits of the dramatic cuts in government spending that are being undertaken across Europe, they are bound to have a significant impact on overall global economic activity and may trigger a double-dip recession, or even – some informed observers think (Krugman 2010) – another Great Depression when combined with the ending of the stimulus in the US. Ironically, governments are hostage to precisely the same sorts of market forces that wreaked such havoc in Asia a decade earlier. Even though the 'efficient markets hypothesis' is now as discredited as the idea that financial innovation is the path to risk diversification,[3] government policy in the West remains especially vulnerable to abrupt shifts in market sentiment and is clearly constructed with this in mind. Paradoxically, though, 'embedded financial orthodoxy' (Cerny 1993) in the form of balanced budgets and 'sound' money may actually exacerbate the problem and trigger the disaster markets fear.

The chances that a coordinated, state-led response to the crisis will occur have been diminished by two other factors. On the one hand, the much-heralded coordinated action that had characterised the meeting of the G20 in the UK following the collapse of Lehman Brothers had largely dissipated by the time the leaders met in Toronto a year later (Beattie 2010). The failure of the most promising part of the putative 'international financial architecture' to agree on a strategy to tackle the crisis was a major blow to both the credibility of the organisation and the prospects for coordinated action. Expectations were further dashed by the European response, which is most directly pertinent when considering East Asia's comparative crisis management.

As the benchmark for regional cooperation and integration, the EU's response to what is arguably its most serious challenge since its foundation had implications for regionalism in other parts of the world. The most striking feature of European action was not simply its ineffective and uncoordinated nature, but the resurgence of national interests and divisions that thwarted it (Stephens 2010b). Real differences emerged between individual states about both the most appropriate policy response, and the degree to which individual members should accept responsibility for the unsustainable, even deceptive nature of their actions. This was most famously highlighted in Germany's reluctance to bail out the profligate Greeks: not only did this highlight the acutely sensitive domestic political consequences that flowed from the crisis, but it also revealed continuing differences between France and Germany over how to deal with a crisis that threatened to get much worse before it got better. It needs to be remembered that the Franco-German accord that underpinned the original implementation of the euro was essentially driven by political rather than economic priorities (Chang 2003); priorities that seemed in danger of being overturned by economic crisis. In short, the very unity and future of the EU appeared to be in serious doubt – a prospect that had hitherto been unimaginable, but which opened a revealing comparative window on East Asia's past and possible future.

In light of the European experience, the prospects for an Asian Currency Unit, which were never bright (Chung and Eichengreen 2007), but which had been occasionally floated by one policy entrepreneur or another, were effectively extinguished. In addition to the formidable technical and political obstacles involved in getting China and Japan to coordinate their policies, let alone the rest of East Asia's highly disparate economies, Europe's crisis suggested it was not a good idea even if it could be achieved. Those sceptics who had always doubted whether a common currency could withstand either a major crisis or the undisciplined behaviour of weaker members appeared to be vindicated: not only had Greek policymakers apparently cooked the books, but they were deprived of the flexibility that a weak currency might have provided when attempting to deal with the crisis. The big lesson about optimum currency areas seemed to be that they were political rather than economic phenomena and that common currencies might cause more problems than they solved (Eichengreen and Frieden 1995). Japan's and China's misgivings about getting too closely integrated with some of their impoverished neighbours suddenly looked judicious and farsighted rather than indecisive and lacking in vision.

But there was and is one other crucial difference between East Asia and Europe, and between the first and second crises, and that is the role played by China. Although a relative bit-player in the first crisis, China has now assumed a starring role and the second crisis might not have occurred at all – or at least, not in quite the way it did – were in not for the part played by China.

China changes everything

China has become the most important trade partners for most of East Asia and this is having a noticeable impact on attitudes toward the PRC as a consequence (Lemoine 2010). But it is China's bilateral relationship with the US which remains pivotal, unparalleled and central to understanding the current crisis. Former US Treasury Secretary Larry Summers (2006) described the relationship between the US and East Asia as the 'balance of financial terror'. This evocative phrase captures something important about the interdependent nature of the contemporary international economy and the vulnerabilities as well as advantages this generates. Simply put, the US and East Asia have for decades developed a symbiotic relationship in which the US has provided a pivotally important market for East Asia's exports, while first Japan and latterly China have obligingly recycled the massive quantities of US dollars they accumulated from their resulting trade surpluses into US government debt. China's and Japan's purchases of US Treasury bonds allowed the US government to maintain low interest and taxation rate regimes, to say nothing of waging costly wars and generally acting like a hegemonic power (Beeson 2009). Without continuing capital inflows of this sort, US primacy may well have been called into question much earlier than it has been. This is what leads some influential observers in the US to argue that Asian states are culpable as they encouraged the US to 'live beyond its means' and were partly responsible for inflating the asset bubbles that have been such central components of the present crisis (Guha 2009).

This structurally embedded relationship has been described by some as 'Bretton Woods II', because of the way it has apparently institutionalised a particular pattern of economic and political relations between East Asia and the US. This symbiotic arrangement is based on what is thought to be an 'unlimited' appetite for US securities because the capacity for growth in East Asia is 'far from its limit' (Dooley et al. 2003). But even before the crisis struck, it was apparent that there were inherent dangers in this relationship, and that there *were* potential limits to the amount of American debt other countries would be willing to absorb (Murphy 2006). In the aftermath of this crisis, it is apparent that that limit may have been reached, as China in particular has reduced the level of its bond purchases (Bradsher 2009). China's foreign policymaking elites have somewhat belatedly recognised the extent of their exposure to America's problems. Not only have some of the direct investments they have made in the US actually lost money (Anderlini 2009a), but there is another potentially more dramatic and problematic aspect to the current crisis that has suddenly come into focus: the US dollar's continuing role as the world's reserve currency means that those countries like China that hold huge reserves of dollars and dollar-denominated assets are effectively hostage to the actions of the US government and the perceptions of international money markets. While the US economy was apparently booming and sucking in imports, China's dependence on the US might have seemed like a sensible strategy and a way of underpinning Chinese exports. Now, however, it looks like dangerous over-exposure and something that urgently needs to be addressed (Wines 2009).

Two aspects of China's response to the crisis and the threat of a dollar devaluation are especially noteworthy in this regard. On the one hand, China's leadership is becoming increasingly outspoken and critical of the US. For example, premier Wen Jiabao directly repudiated the idea that China contributed to the crisis, claiming that it stemmed from an

> excessive expansion of financial institutions in blind pursuit of profit, lack of self-discipline among financial institutions and rating agencies [and] the failure of financial supervision and regulation to keep up with financial innovations which allowed the risks of financial derivatives to build and spread. (Quoted in Tett and Edgecliffe-Johnson 2009)

Given this growing assertiveness and the analysis of the crisis that underpinned it, the widely noted remarks of Zhou Xiaochuan, Governor of the People's Bank of China, were especially significant. Zhou (2009) argued that the international monetary system needed to be reformed and an international reserve currency should be created that was 'disconnected from individual nations'. Although Zhou did not mention the US directly, the implication is clear; China wants to be one of the driving forces shaping any post-crisis international order. However, China's ambitions and growing international status may make its regional relations more problematic. Significantly, Wen suggested that the G7 could be an appropriate forum for discussions about the new order, and Zhou argued for a greater role for the IMF – an institution over which China is keen to enhance its influence. Neither Wen nor Zhou mentioned East Asian institutions. Indeed, many observers think that ultimately a 'G2' composed of China and the US will be the defining part of whatever institutional architecture emerges in the aftermath of the crisis (Brzezinski 2009). The question in such circumstances is whether China's international and regional roles are compatible.

As far as the East Asian region is concerned, therefore, the second crisis has produced contradictory outcomes, largely as a consequence of China's growing importance. The rapid economic growth and increased political prominence that have made China such an important regional actor have also enhanced its global role. On the one hand this has meant that China's relationships with East Asia have become more important to its trade partners and generally improved as a result. On the other hand, however, the importance of China's bilateral relationship with the US means that the significance of the region may be diminished. The source of China's enhanced importance at both the regional and global level is, of course, its unprecedented economic development. As a consequence, the debate about 'decoupling', which was such a prominent part of the early phase of the latest crisis, is of more than academic interest.

The decoupling thesis had suggested that China (and by extension the rest of East Asia) were increasingly self-reliant, and immune to the vicissitudes of economic activity in the US – hitherto the global economy's principal growth engine and pivotal part of the entire East Asian developmental experience. If China's economy had become large enough to act as a regional source of economic expansion, its regional importance would be entrenched and its immunity to US pressure would be more assured. At this stage the signals are mixed: certainly, China has been able to resist American pressure to allow the renminbi to float, and its massive domestic stimulus package has kept both its own and the region's economies expanding. Indeed, the very fact that China had both the wherewithal and the governance structure that allowed it to rapidly implement such a stimulus stands in striking contrast with the US where the process was more politically controversial and achieved with borrowed money. On the other hand, though, many observers are concerned about the unproductive nature of some of the domestic investment that has occurred in China and the possible fragility of some aspects of the domestic economy, such as the banking and real estate sectors (Anderlini 2009b). The stakes could hardly be higher for China's ruling elites: not only was the health of the economy and thus the geopolitical position of the Chinese state on the line, but so too was the fate of the regime itself. As David Lampton (2008: 144) points out, 'regime legitimacy in China currently rests on two pillars – rapid economic growth and vigorous defense of nationalistic values'. These plainly have the capacity to interact in unpredictable ways in the event of a downturn in China itself.

Comparative implications

The first crisis of globalisation had the effect of galvanising regional development in East Asia. The region's political elites recognised their collective vulnerability and attempted to develop strategies and modes of cooperation that would leave them less exposed and vulnerable to future economic upheavals. Unsurprisingly, given the particular nature of the first crisis, the principal focus of attention was financial sector reform and the development of monetary regionalism. In retrospect it is evident that, while the extent of the collaboration has been modest, the creation of defence mechanisms in the form of currency reserves inadvertently created the preconditions for a new crisis, albeit one with its epicentre elsewhere. One of the principal reasons that regional collaboration has not gone further, faster, has been an absence of effective and undisputed leadership at a regional level. Japan attempted but failed, while China was not in a position to offer real leadership – especially given its own continuing rivalry with Japan. Indeed, little more than a decade ago, China was effectively a bystander and a limited force in regional and global politics.

A number of things have happened since the first crisis that have fundamentally changed the dynamics of the second. First, this is a truly global crisis and one centred on the US rather than East Asia. Although East Asia's investments in the US may have helped create the preconditions for the present crisis, thus far Asian economies have emerged relatively unscathed. Indeed, the second striking feature of the current crisis is that China in particular has become a much more important and assertive power. China's rapidly growing economic significance and a greater willingness to play the sort of international role that goes with it has necessarily given its policymakers a focus that transcends the region. For China, political, economic and strategic imperatives mean that the relationship with the US – now unambiguously the single most important bilateral relationship in the world – will inevitably take precedence over narrowly defined regional issues. Consequently, the prospects for regionalism this time round may be rather different. Whereas the first crisis was ultimately positive and integrative for East Asia, the second may have the opposite effect. The tensions generated in Europe and the possible limitations of monetary cooperation that have been so graphically highlighted there may well have the same sorts of demonstration effects that European integration has had more generally.

In other words, the pace of greater political and economic integration in Asia may slow as a consequence of this crisis, especially given the absence of established and effective regional mechanisms with which to coordinate any collective response.

So what are the major lessons that emerge from a comparison of these two quite different crises? For students of regionalism perhaps the biggest lesson is that crises can have centrifugal as well as centripetal effects. Clearly, much depends on the way policymakers interpret and try to respond to crises, but the fact that the putative leaders of East Asia were not as responsible for the economic fates of their neighbours as their European counterparts meant that expectations about East Asian regionalism were modest. In Europe, by contrast, the inability of the EU's elaborate, highly institutionalised structures of governance to cope with a major crisis has left the entire European project looking surprisingly uncertain. Having said that, it is not obvious where East Asian regional cooperation goes from here either: the European experience is likely to dampen enthusiasm for deeper monetary cooperation; China's growing global role is likely to limit the attention it gives to purely regional issues. Consequently, East Asia may still find itself lacking an obvious leader or even the sort of Franco-German condominium that has driven European integration.

Perhaps the most important and revealing change in the international system that was thrown into stark relief by the two crises was the diminished role of the US. Even though it is clear in retrospect that the relative position of the US was neither as dominant nor as assured as many assumed in the late 1990s, by 2010 the extent of American decline was becoming unambiguously apparent (Pape 2009). The duration and scale of the economic downturn in the US, the reliance of the American government on continuing inflows of capital from China, the loss of authority and confidence in Anglo-American capitalism, and the increasingly toxic, dysfunctional nature of its domestic politics, led some observers to speculate that the US might experience a dramatic fall from its pre-eminent position of the last 50 years or so (Ferguson 2010b). In such circumstances, the possibility that the world's financial architecture might actually be reformed at either the regional or the global level in ways that would make a third crisis unlikely if not impossible look as remote as ever.

Notes

1 LTCM's strategy of fixed income arbitrage came unstuck when the Russian government defaulted on its loans in the wake of the Asian crisis, revealing LTCM as highly leveraged, unable to meet its obligations, and triggering a bail-out of the sort that has become so familiar in the latest crisis (see Lowenstein 2001).

2 This is not to say that no one raised the alarm. On the contrary, a number of observers pointed to the potentially unsustainable nature of economic development in the US, but such views were largely marginalised (see, for example, Brenner 2002).

3 Perhaps the most significant point in this context is not that this thesis exercised such a surprising influence for so long, but the underlying role played by the economics profession in uncritically legitimising a narrow set of abstractions that were at odds with empirical historical reality (see Colander et al. 2009).

References

Altman, R. C. (2009) 'Globalization in retreat', *Foreign Affairs* 88: 2–7.

Anderlini, J. (2009a) 'China lost billions in diversity drive', *Financial Times*, 15 March.

Anderlini, J. (2009b) 'Beijing's stimulus measures questioned'. *Financial Times*, 18 May.

Armijo, L. E. (2001) 'The political geography of world financial reform: who wants what and why?', *Global Governance* 7: 379–96.

Beattie, A. (2010) 'G20 unity frays as states go own way', *Financial Times*, 22 June.

Beeson, M. (2006) 'American hegemony and regionalism: the rise of East Asia and the end of the Asia-Pacific', *Geopolitics* 11(4): 541–60.

Beeson, M. (2007) *Regionalism and Globalization in East Asia: Politics, Security, and Economic Development*, Basingstoke: Palgrave Macmillan.

Beeson, M. (2009) 'Hegemonic transition in East Asia? The dynamics of Chinese and American power', *Review of International Studies* 35(1): 95–112.

Beeson, M. and Broome, A. (2010) 'Hegemonic instability and East Asia: contradictions, crises and US power', *Globalizations* 7(4): 479–95.

Bhagwati, J. (1998) 'The capital myth', *Foreign Affairs* 77(3): 7–12.

Blackburn, R. (2008) 'The subprime crisis', *New Left Review* 50(March–April): 63–106.

Bradsher, K. (2009) 'China losing taste for debt from the U.S.', *New York Times*, 8 January.

Brenner, R. (2002) *The Boom and the Bubble*, London: Verso.

Brzezinski, Z. (2009) 'The Group of Two that could change the world', *Financial Times*, 13 January.

Brown, G. (2007) *Speech by the Chancellor of the Exchequer*, Mansion House, London; accessed at http://www.hm-treasury.gov.uk/press_68_07.htm. Accessed 1 April 2008.

Cerny, P. G. (1993) 'American decline and the emergence of embedded financial orthodoxy', in P. G. Cerny (ed.) *Finance and World Politics: Markets, Regimes and States in the Post-hegemonic Era*, Aldershot: Edward Elgar, pp. 155–85.

Chang, H.-J. (2000) 'The hazard of moral hazard: Untangling the Asian crisis', *World Development* 28(4): 775–8.

Chang, M. (2003) 'Franco-German interests in European monetary integration', in J. Kirshner (ed.) *Monetary Orders: Ambiguous Economics, Ubiquitous Politics*, Ithaca, NY: Cornell University Press, pp. 218–35.

Chung, D. and Eichengreen, B. (2007) 'Exchange rate arrangements for emerging East Asia', in D. Chung and B. Eichengreen (eds) *Toward an East Asian Exchange Rate Regime*, Washington: Brookings Institution, pp. 1–21.

Colander, D., Goldberg, M., Haas, A., Juselius, K., Kirman, A., Lux, T. and Sloth, B. (2009) 'The financial crisis and the systemic failure of the economics profession', *Critical Review: A Journal of Politics and Society* 21(2): 249–67.

Crotty, J. (2009) 'Structural causes of the global financial crisis: a critical assessment of the "new financial architecture"', *Cambridge Journal of Economics* 33: 563–80.

Dieter, H. (2008) 'ASEAN and the emerging monetary regionalism: a case of limited contribution', *The Pacific Review* 21(4): 489–506.
Dooley, M. P., Folkerts-Landau, D. and Garber, P. (2003) 'An essay on the revived Bretton Woods system', *Working Paper 9971*, Cambridge, MA: National Bureau of Economic Research.
Eichengreen, B. and Frieden, J. (1995) 'The political economy of European monetary unification: an analytical introduction', in B. Eichengreen and J. Frieden (eds) *The Political Economy of European Monetary Unification*, The Hague: Kluwer Law International, pp. 1–23.
Elliott, L. and Atkinson, D. (2008) *The Gods That Failed: How Blind Faith in Markets Has Cost Us Our Future*, London: Bodley Head.
Ferguson, N. (2010a) 'Today's Keynesians have learnt nothing', *Financial Times*, 19 July.
Ferguson, N. (2010b) 'Complexity and collapse', *Foreign Affairs* 89(2): 18–32.
Foster, J. B. and Magdoff, F. (2009) *The Great Financial Crisis: Causes and Consequences*, New York: Monthly Review Press.
Grimes, W. W. (2006) 'East Asian financial regionalism in support of the global financial architecture? The political economy of regional nesting', *Journal of East Asian Studies* 6: 353–80.
Grimes, W. W. (2009) *Currency and Contest in East Asia: The Great Power Politics of Financial Regionalism*, Ithaca, NY: Cornell University Press.
Guha, K. (2009) 'Paulson says crisis sown by imbalance', *Financial Times*, 1 January.
Hall, R. B. (2003) 'The discursive demolition of the Asian development model', *International Studies Quarterly* 47(1): 71–99.
Higgott, R. (2000) 'The international relations of the Asian economic crisis', in R. Robison et al. (eds) *Politics and Markets in the Wake of the Asian Crisis*, London: Routledge, pp. 261–82.
Jacobs, L. and King, D. (2009) 'America's political crisis: the unsustainable state in a time of unraveling', *PS: Political Science and Politics* 42(2): 277–85.
Johnson, S. (2009) 'The quiet coup', *The Atlantic Monthly* (May).
Kindleberger, C. P. (1973) *The World in Depression 1929–1939*, Berkley: University of California Press.
Krugman, P. (2009) 'America the tarnished', *New York Times*, 30 March.
Krugman, P. (2010) 'The third depression', *New York Times*, 27 June.
Lampton, D. M. (2008) *The Three Faces of Chinese Power: Might, Money, and Minds*, Berkeley: University of California Press.
Lardy, N. R. (2002) *Integrating China into the Global Economy*, Washington: Brookings Institute.
Lee, Y. W. (2006) 'Japan and the Asian Monetary Fund: an identity-intention approach', *International Studies Quarterly* 50: 339–66.
Lemoine, F. (2010) 'Past successes and new challenges: China's foreign trade at a turning point', *China and World Economy* 18: 1–23.
Lowenstein, R. (2001) *When Genius Failed: The Rise and Fall of Long-Term Capital Management*, New York: Random House.
Murphy, R. T. (2006) 'East Asia's dollars', *New Left Review* 40: 39–64.
Panitch, L. and Gindin, S. (2004) 'Finance and American empire', in L. Panitch and C. Leys (eds) *The Socialist Register: The Empire Reloaded*, London: Merlin Press, pp. 46–80.
Pape, R. A. (2009) 'Empire falls', *National Interest* (99): 21–34.
Ravenhill, J. (2002) 'A three bloc world? The new East Asian regionalism', *International Relations of the Asia Pacific* 2(2): 167–95.
Reich, R. (2010) 'The Senate finance bill merits two cheers', *Financial Times*, 23 May.

Reinhart, C. M. and Rogoff, K. S. (2009) *This Time Is Different: Eight Centuries of Financial Folly*, Princeton, NJ: Princeton University Press.
Soederberg, S. (2001) 'The Emperor's new suit: the new international financial architecture as a reinvention of the Washington Consensus', *Global Governance* 7: 453–67.
Stephens, P. (2010a) 'Three years on, the markets are masters again', *Financial Times*, 30 July.
Stephens, P. (2010b) 'Europe unravels in a tangle of national interests', *Financial Times*, 29 April.
Summers, L. H. (2006) 'Reflections on global account imbalances in emerging markets reserve accumulation', L. K. Jha Memorial Lecture, Mumbai India.
Tett, G. (2009) *Fool's Gold: How Unrestrained Greed Corrupted a Dream, Shattered Global Markets and Unleashed a Catastrophe*, London, Little, Brown.
Tett, G. and Edgecliffe-Johnson, A. (2009) 'Wen blames crisis on policy mistakes', *Financial Times*, 28 January.
The Economist (2010) 'East or famine', 25 February.
Vasudevan, R. (2009) 'Dollar hegemony, financialization, and the credit crisis', *Review of Radical Political Economics* 41(3): 291–304.
Vermeiren, M. (2010) 'The global imbalances and the contradictions of US monetary hegemony', *Journal of International Relations and Development* 13(2): 105–35.
Wade, R. (2000) 'Wheels within wheels: rethinking the Asian crisis and the Asian model', *Annual Review of Political Science* 3: 85–115.
Wang, H. (2003) 'China's exchange rate policy in the aftermath of the Asian financial crisis', in J. Kirshner (ed.) *Monetary Orders: Ambiguous Economics, Ubiquitous Politics*, Ithaca, NY: Cornell University Press, pp. 153–71.
Wines, M. (2009) 'China's leader says he is "worried" over U.S. Treasuries', *New York Times*, 14 March.
Wolf, M. (2009) 'Why Obama's new Tarp will fail to rescue the banks', *Financial Times*, 10 February.
Wolf, M. (2010) 'A bail-out for Greece is just the beginning', *Financial Times*, 4 May.
Zhao, S. (2010) 'The China model: can it replace the Western model of modernization?', *Journal of Contemporary China* 19(65): 419–36.
Zhou Xiaochuan (2009) 'Reform the international monetary system', People's Bank of China, accessed at http://www.pbc.gov.cn/english//detail.asp?col=6500&ID=178

Afterword

Saori N. Katada

Since the summer of 2011, when *The Pacific Review* published this collection of studies on the impact of the Global Financial Crisis (GFC) on East Asian regionalism, the world has faced with the renewed worries about the double dip recession. Europe, on the one hand, is facing the euro crisis as the Greek sovereign debt restructuring hits deadlock, and the fear of the crisis has continued to mount leading to the interest rates on the Italian and Spanish bonds to rise to a record high. On the other hand, the political gridlock over extension of the US government debt ceiling led Standard & Poor's to downgrade the credit rating of the US Federal government on August 5, 2011, to below triple A for the first time in history. These jitters amidst the prolonged recession on both sides of the North Atlantic Ocean struck home that the GFC was far from over. In a stark contrast, the economic recovery in East Asia after the GFC has been robust. Now as an unprecedented move, the European Union targeted China's hefty and increasing foreign exchange reserves as it requested the Chinese government to pitch in to support European debt restructuring to calm the euro crisis.

Advances in East Asian regionalism remain precarious, however. On the monetary and financial front, the euro crisis has hit home to the already reluctant monetary authorities in the region that the common currency is nothing but a straightjacket that restricts the governments' policy autonomy in tackling urgent financial and fiscal problems. Despite the successful establishment of the ASEAN Macroeconomic Research Office (AMRO) in Singapore early 2011, the East Asian financial arrangement remains limited and it will continue to rely on the IMF. In addition, the newly enhanced bilateral currency swap mechanisms among China, Japan and South Korea in October 2011 have raised concerns regarding the intensions of the large creditor country in securing the financial stability of the entire region. With G20 bogged down by the euro crisis, East Asian governments seem to have lost any convergence point in addressing global monetary issues. Hence the East Asian governments continue to rely on the dollar and pump their foreign exchange reserves into the US Treasury Bills despite all the worries of declining dollar and creditworthiness of its government's debts.

On the trade front, a consolidated regional arrangement is yet to emerge. The FTA (free trade agreement) picture has become even more complex during the last year as the need for solid economic recovery led the Obama administration to court much more decidedly the dynamic East Asian economies. After ratifying the long-pending FTA with Korea in October 2011, the US government hosted the APEC Summit in Hawaii in November 2011 where a framework agreement for the Trans-Pacific Partnership Agreement (TPP) was reached, and where Japan made the historic announcement to participate. In pursuit of a "high quality" FTA, which in principle will tolerate no sector exclusions, the TPP currently with nine negotiating members (Singapore, New Zealand, Chile, Brunei, Australia, Peru, Vietnam, Malaysia and the United States) and three countries seeking admission (Japan, Canada and Mexico) is like to expand even further around the Pacific Rim. For the first time ever, the United States President also attended the East Asian Summit in Indonesia (November 17, 2011) sending a message of much deeper U.S. engagement in the region. Uncomfortable with the sense of economic containment, the Chinese government has buttressed its pursuit of the FTA among China, Japan and Korea (CJK), with leaders from the three countries announcing that they are ready to move soon from the joint study to the actual negotiation stage. Furthermore, the ASEAN nations responded to the heightened interests in the TPP by agreeing to be on board with the Japan-proposed Comprehensive Economic Partnership for East Asia (CEPEA) that includes ASEAN+6 (China, Japan, South Korea, Australia, New Zealand, and India) countries. All this fluidity in the regional preferential trade arrangements attests to our claim that the ground for East Asian regionalism continues to shift.

The rise of China continues to influence the regional and global economic debates. The U.S. government maintains the pressure towards China's currency revaluation, as the United States launches its export offensive. As the European economy goes through significant contraction, China's export interests will focus more on the Pacific than ever before. Seen as the engine of not only the regional but also the global economic recovery, the hope and pressure put on the Chinese economy mounts. For the better or for worse, such dynamics surrounding East Asia prevent the region from turning inward. With demonstrated economic and security interests of the United States in the region, the GFC might have placed East Asia in the center of the global economic map, though still without regional coherence or strategy.

Index

Page numbers in *Italics* represent tables.
Page numbers in **Bold** represent figures.